DNA
FINGERPRINTING

THE ULTIMATE IDENTITY

DNA
FINGERPRINTING
THE ULTIMATE IDENTITY

RON FRIDELL

FRANKLIN WATTS
A Division of Scholastic Inc.
New York • Toronto • London • Auckland • Sydney
Mexico City • New Delhi • Hong Kong
Danbury, Connecticut

Interior layout by Jeff Loppacker

Cover photograph ©: Photo Researchers: Dr. Kari Lounatmaa/SPL.

Photographs ©: AP/Wide World Photos: 61 (Karen Tam), 85; Archive Photos: 24 (David McNew/Reuters), 48 (Sam Mircovich/Reuters), 88; Corbis-Bettmann: 8 bottom (SPL), 8 top (Jim Zuckerman), 86; Custom Medical Stock Photo: 23 (Wedgworth), 32; Liaison Agency, Inc.: 67 (Stephen Ferry), 58 (Jonathan Levine), 76 (Kevin Moloney); Peter Arnold Inc.: 94 (Leonard Lessin); Photo Researchers: 34 (Neville Chadwick/SPL), 19 top (James King-Holmes/SPL), 78 (Jeff Lepore), 17 (Matt Meadows/SPL), 16 (David Parker/SPL), 96 (Art Stein); PhotoEdit: 19 bottom (Laura Dwight); Stock Boston: 20 (Jim Whitmer); The Stock Shop: 82 (Messerschmidt); Stone: 13 (Bob Torrez); Superstock, Inc.: 91; The Image Works: 79 (James Marshall).

Visit Franklin Watts on the Internet at:
http://publishing.grolier.com

Library of Congress Cataloging-in-Publication Data

Fridell, Ron
    DNA fingerprinting: the ultimate identity / Ron Fridell
        p. cm.
    Includes bibliographical references and index.
    Summary: Discusses the discovery of DNA fingerprinting, the processes involved, its initial use, and its past and present role in forensic identification, conservation biology, and human genetics.
    ISBN 0-531-11858-4
    1. DNA fingerprinting—Juvenile literature. [1. DNA fingerprinting. 2. Forensic sciences.] I. Title.
RA1057.55.F75 2001
614'.1—dc21
                                        00-026925

Contents

TWO KINDS OF FINGERPRINTS

Imagine putting a letter into an envelope and then licking the flap and sealing it. You have just left behind two kinds of fingerprints.

The first kind, *digital fingerprints*, came from the raised ridges of skin that run in patterns of curving lines along the tips of your fingers and thumbs. You left them all over the letter and envelope. No one else on Earth could have made those digital fingerprints. Each one is unique to you.

The second kind, *DNA fingerprints*, came from your saliva when you licked the flap. Those DNA fingerprints also are unique to you, but they are not fingerprints that you can see or touch. Where are these unique patterns? They are in your *DNA*.

What DNA Looks Like

DNA, or deoxyribonucleic acid, is found in nearly every single one of the more than 75 trillion *cells* that make up the human body. DNA is embedded in our skin cells and our hair roots and our saliva. It's in our blood, our sweat, and our tears. To see what this DNA looks like, we need to take a close look inside a typical human cell. To do this, we must use an electron microscope, which magnifies the cell millions of times.

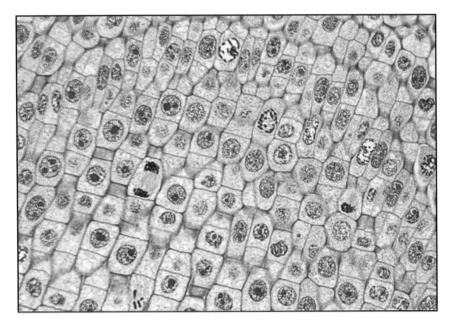

DNA is found in almost every human cell, including skin and blood. A light microscope is used to look at the skin cells (top). A scanning electron microscope shows the surface of blood cells (bottom).

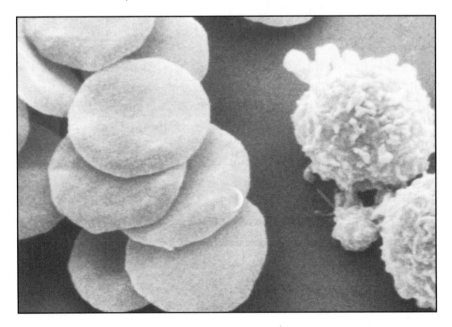

Within this highly magnified cell, 46 *chromosomes* float in a watery nucleus. These threadlike strands are made of *protein* and DNA *molecules*. A close look at one of these DNA molecules reveals what scientists call the double helix. This large, double-stranded molecule resembles a long, spiraling ladder. The two sides of this spiraling DNA ladder are made of four building blocks called *nucleotides*. Each nucleotide is made of a sugar joined to a *phosphate* and a base. These bases come in four varieties. Scientists have identified them by the letters A (*adenine*), C (*cytosine*), G (*guanine*), and T (*thymine*), the four letters that make up the DNA alphabet.

These nucleotides are arranged in *base pairs*, with each pair making up a rung on the DNA ladder. Nucleotides pair up according to strict rules. Nucleotide A pairs only with nucleotide T, and nucleotide G pairs only with nucleotide C. The A–T and G–C base pairs, repeated in various sequences again and again, make up the 3 billion "rungs" of the DNA ladder. These base pairs are arranged in a very specific order called the *DNA sequence*.

What DNA Does

Scientists have compared the DNA sequence to the letters that make up the words in a book of instructions. The experts have also compared it to the software that programs computers. What is it about DNA that makes them think this way?

It turns out that the DNA molecules in a single cell—the basic unit of living matter—carry within them all the vital information and instructions needed for growth and operation of a human being. Because of DNA, our cells divide to produce more cells. Because of DNA, our hearts beat, our lungs breathe, our ears hear, and our eyes see. Because of DNA, our bodies live, grow, and function. In this way, we can say that everyone is programmed by DNA from the moment of conception.

The DNA sequence in each of our cells carries the hereditary information transmitted to us from our parents. The chromosomes

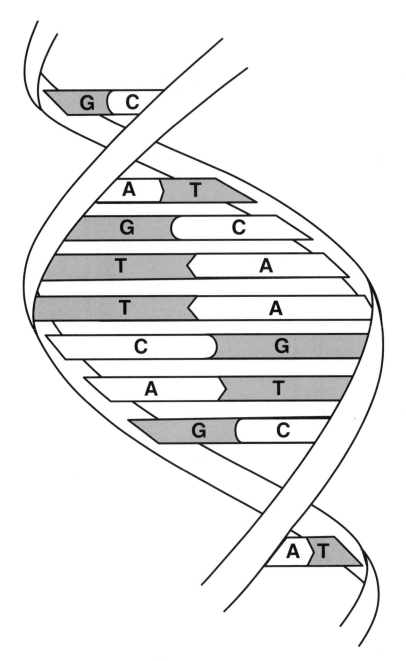

The sides of DNA form a twisted ladder. The "rungs" are composed of nucleotide bases—adenine (A) always binds to thymine (T), and guanine (G) always binds to cytosine (C).

in the nucleus, or control center, of each cell contain the information. These 46 chromosomes come in two sets, each with 23 chromosomes. One set is inherited from our father, and the other set is inherited from our mother. This information determines what we will grow up to look like. Our DNA determines our hair color, eye color, skin color, and height. DNA also determines the physical characteristics we all have in common, such as two eyes, two arms, and two legs.

The DNA sequence within each of our cells also carries the operating manual that tells our bodies how to grow and function. These instructions are packaged in units called *genes*. Each gene consists of one small section of the DNA ladder. (A typical gene takes up about 3,000 of the 3 billion "rungs" of the DNA ladder.)

Each gene has its own special task to perform. The gene's DNA code, which is made up of sequences of A–T and G–C nucleotide base pairs, "tells" the gene to produce one specific kind of protein. Proteins are the body's building blocks. Together, all the genes produce the thousands of different kinds of proteins that make up the cells and *tissues* of the human body. All the genes in a cell—80,000 or so—make up the human *genome*, the coded genetic blueprint that is contained in virtually every one of the more than 75 trillion cells in the human body.

Chapter 1

DISCOVERY

Similar but Different

The coded instructions in your genome are almost identical to the instructions in everyone else's genome. This makes sense, because every member of the species *Homo sapiens* looks and functions a great deal like another. Each of us has one head, two eyes, two ears, one nose, a neck between the head and shoulders, and so on. Each of us has a throat that swallows, lungs that breathe, and blood that flows.

But your genome is not quite identical to anyone else's. Small but significant differences in the DNA sequence appear here and there along the DNA ladder. Here's how a *geneticist*, a scientist who studies genes, explains these differences to a lecture audience:

> Look at the neighbor to your left and to your right. You're 99.9 percent identical. But in a genome of 3 billion letters, even a tenth of a percent difference translates into 3 million separate spelling differences. I invite you again to look to the left and look to the right and notice how unique you are. There is no one in this audience who has the same DNA sequence as anyone else.[1]

None of these teenagers looks exactly the same, and none of them shares the same DNA sequence.

This geneticist is referring to 3 million of the 3 billion rungs on the DNA ladder—a tiny fraction of the total DNA. The 3 million rungs where the greatest differences appear are scattered in separate regions here and there throughout the genome. The regions showing the most extreme variation are called *polymorphic regions*. These polymorphic regions are made up of short bursts of stuttered, or repeated, sequences of nucleotide base pairs, 3 to 20 base pairs long, repeated over and over again. These regions of DNA are not actually involved in the production of proteins. They have no known use.

Because these parts of DNA don't seem useful, scientists sometimes refer to them as "junk DNA." But while studying these polymorphic regions, one scientist made a startling discovery—he found out how to make DNA fingerprints.

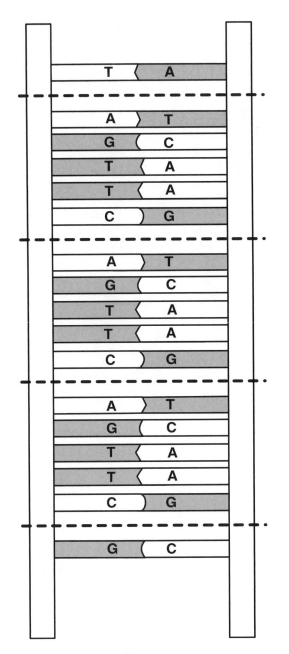

Scientists call a DNA repeating sequence such as the one pictured here a polymorphic region. This one is made up of three repeated sequences of five base pairs.

Reading the Blueprint

When people read a book, they look at the order of words in a sentence and make sense of them. Scientists had tried, without much success, to "read" the polymorphic regions of the DNA ladder. They wanted to look at the order of the base pairs as they do when they open a book and look at the order of the words. Part of the problem was location. With these polymorphic regions scattered here and there throughout the genome, how could scientists find them easily?

One geneticist, an Englishman named Alec Jeffreys, was working on the problem. He had become interested in science as a boy. "My interest in genetics and *biochemistry* began at the age of seven," he says, "when my father presented me with a microscope and a remarkably lethal chemistry set. I followed this growing interest in chemistry and biology throughout my school days and became particularly interested in the interface between the two subjects."[2] This interface, or point of connection, is the science of biochemistry.

Jeffreys studied biochemistry at Oxford University in Oxford, England. After completing his studies in 1975, he began doing research on the subject of mammalian molecular genetics, the gene structure of mammals. This research led to an interest in the gene structure of humans, particularly those polymorphic regions where the DNA sequence varies most from person to person.

"People had already stumbled over several of these stuttered regions of DNA purely by accident," Jeffreys said. "We wanted to find a way to get to them any time we wanted." Jeffreys wondered whether it was possible to identify individual people by their DNA sequence. After all, he reasoned, "DNA is the ultimate level of inherited variation. You cannot get more fundamental a variation than in DNA itself."[3]

While working in his laboratory at Leicester University in Leicester, England, Jeffreys made a startling discovery about how to "read" the structure of human DNA. First, using a sample of

Alec Jeffreys with two sets of DNA fingerprints

human blood, he managed to isolate DNA molecules from blood cells. Then, using a special *restriction enzyme* to bring about a chemical reaction, he managed to chop these DNA molecules into fragments of different lengths, which he then stored on a blot made of nylon membrane.

So far, Jeffreys was using techniques that had been developed by other scientists. What he did next, though, was revolutionary. Jeffreys developed a new tool for locating the polymorphic regions. "If we developed a chemical probe which could latch on to this chemical motif [repeated pattern] that was shared between different stuttered regions in a person's DNA—called *minisatellites*—we could isolate a lot of stuttered DNA regions at once and thereby develop good markers for genetic analysis."[4]

Jeffreys' revolutionary minisatellites were short fragments of DNA that had been chopped out of these polymorphic regions. Why did he call them *minisatellites?* They were small and they surrounded the part of the gene that carries the vital operating instructions for producing proteins.

Then Jeffreys used a *radioisotope* to make minisatellite probes radioactive. That way, he could track them and take pictures of them with X-ray film. Jeffreys had designed each of these radioactive fragments of DNA to operate like a homing device. He would send the probe out along the genome's twisted ladder, where it would keep moving until it reached one of these minisatellite

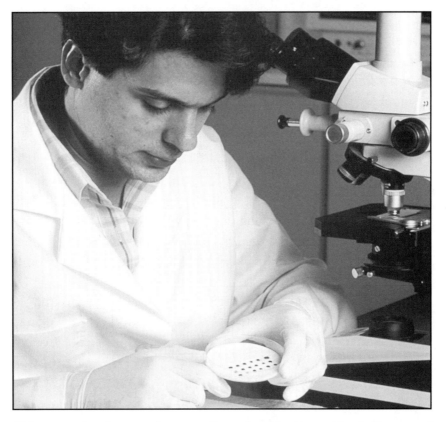

This researcher is preparing genetic probes like those Alec Jeffreys used to find matching DNA fragments and make the first DNA fingerprint.

polymorphic regions. The probe would stop when it came to a fragment of DNA with a sequence of A–T and G–C base pairs identical to its own—a twin. The minisatellite probe would then bind to the twin.

Jeffreys applied a number of radioactive minisatellite probes to the human DNA on the blot. Wherever one would bind, another small part of this polymorphic region of the genome would be captured. Jeffreys would then take an X-ray photograph of the results. Each radioactive probe, along with its twin, would show up as a band on the film. The more of these bands that showed up, the more of the uncharted regions of the genome would be revealed.

The First DNA Fingerprint

On the morning of September 15, 1984, Jeffreys pulled the X-ray film from the developing tank and laid it out for himself and his research assistants to examine. They peered down at the film with great interest but without much hope. The best they could realistically expect were a few isolated glimpses of these mysterious, uncharted regions of the DNA genome.

What they saw was something else entirely. Jeffreys remembers the moment distinctly: "I pulled the X-ray film out of the developing tank and thought, 'Oh God, what have we done here?' "[5]

Jeffreys' minisatellite probes had located many more matches in the target DNA sample than he and his research assistants could have predicted. Instead of a few isolated images of a polymorphic DNA region, they saw long strings of images arranged in patterns. Dark bands—some thick, some thin—were stacked in patterns that looked a great deal like the bar codes found on products in the supermarkets. These patterns of bands, Jeffreys soon realized, represented something hugely important and completely unexpected.

"It was a classic case of basic science coming up with a technology that could be applied to a problem in an unanticipated

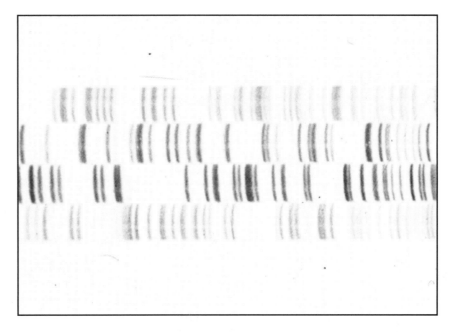

The DNA fingerprint shown at the top looks much like the bar code on the package at the bottom.

way," Jeffreys said. "We'd been looking for good genetic markers for basic genetic analysis and had stumbled on a way of establishing a human's genetic identification."[6]

Using the minisatellite probes, Jeffreys had unlocked the secret of how to reveal the mysterious polymorphic regions of the human genome so that they could be photographed and classified in great detail. He called this process *restriction fragment length polymorphism* (RFLP). And he called the result a "DNA fingerprint." Why? The patterns of base pairs in the polymorphic regions, like the patterns of skin ridges in digital fingerprints, are distinctive and different in each and every human being on the planet.

But unlike digital fingerprints, which are found only on the tips of the fingers and thumbs, DNA fingerprints are found in virtually every one of the more than 75 trillion cells in the human body. And these patterns are exactly alike in each and every cell of one person. This isn't surprising, because all the cells in an individual person originate from one fertilized egg. But Jeffreys had to be absolutely certain, so he tested all kinds of human cells—blood cells, skin cells, hair cells, saliva cells, semen cells, urine cells, and bone cells. They all produced the same unique pattern of markings in these polymorphic regions of the genome.

These tests proved that a person's DNA fingerprint is the same no matter what kind of cell it comes from. They also demonstrated that a DNA fingerprint, just like a

All human beings except identical twins have unique DNA fingerprints.

digital fingerprint, is unique to that person and that person alone. Your DNA fingerprint, Jeffreys said, "does not belong to anyone on the face of this planet who ever has been or ever will be."[7] Identical twins are the only exception.

Inspiration and Discovery

Meanwhile, another scientist on another continent had discovered a new technique that would revolutionize the process of DNA fingerprinting. His name was Kary Mullis. Like Alec Jeffreys, Mullis was a highly educated scientist. He received his Ph.D. in biochemistry from the University of California at Berkeley. And like Jeffreys, Mullis was concentrating on the structure of human genes.

Scientists come in all sorts of shapes and sizes with all sorts of different personalities and world views. Unlike Jeffreys, Mullis did not have the patience and dedication for doing extensive laboratory research work. "I like writing about biology, not doing it," Mullis said. And unlike the quiet and hardworking Jeffreys, Mullis craved fame and publicity. "I love a microphone and a big crowd; I'm an entertainer, I guess."[8] Scientific discoveries are made in different ways. Alec Jeffreys' discovery came to him after long hours in the laboratory physically manipulating bits and pieces of human tissue. Mullis was miles away from any laboratory when he made his discovery.

Just before making his DNA discovery, Mullis worked as a lab technician, making short chains of DNA for other scientists to work with. Mullis found this lab work routine and tedious, but it helped direct his thinking. It made him question the methods used in his work. Wasn't there a faster, more efficient way to analyze DNA samples?

One night in 1983, Mullis discovered this method. The solution came to him all at once as he was mentally manipulating ideas. The way Mullis describes it, he was driving along a California highway when the inspiration came to him. He quickly pulled over to the side of the road, grabbed an envelope and a pencil from the glove compartment, and jotted down calculation after calculation. He didn't stop until he was satisfied that, as he put it, "I had just solved the two major problems in DNA chemistry. Abundance and distinction. And I had done it in one stroke."[9]

By "abundance," Mullis meant the problem of trying to analyze tiny samples of DNA. With Mullis's new method at their disposal, scientists could now have as much DNA material to work with as they wanted, even if all they had to start with was a single cell. By "distinction," he meant that these copies would always be the same size and sequence—a perfectly accurate copy of the original sample.

Another Method of DNA Fingerprinting

Mullis called his new technique of copying DNA molecules *PCR,* which stands for *polymerase chain reaction.* The key ingredient in the PCR technique is an enzyme, a protein that speeds up chemical reactions. This enzyme, called *Taq DNA polymerase,* comes from bacteria found in geysers and hot springs. Taq DNA polymerase is a remarkably hardy enzyme. It can survive in temperatures approaching the boiling point of water—the same temperatures required to take apart or "unzip" the double-stranded DNA molecules to prepare them for copying.

Some people have called PCR analysis "molecular Xeroxing" because it can create unlimited copies of very small sections of DNA very quickly. Each copying cycle takes only a matter of minutes. The one copy of DNA from a single cell becomes 2 copies, 2 become 4, 4 become 8, 8 become 16, and so on. Twenty cycles yield a million copies, 30 cycles a billion. Scientists use a machine called a thermal cycler to produce these copies. It takes about 3 hours to make a billion copies of a single DNA molecule.

The PCR process itself is not DNA fingerprinting—it is a technique used to increase the amount of DNA available for testing. In cases where not enough DNA is available for RFLP testing, scientists can perform special PCR-based tests using DNA copies produced by the PCR technique.

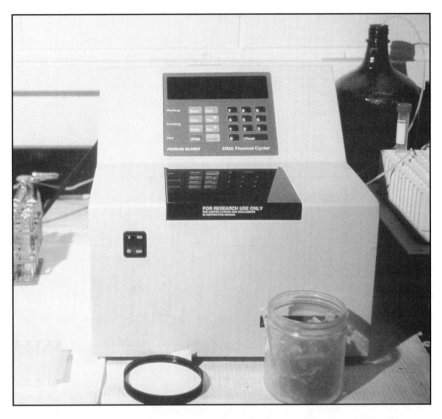

Scientists use a thermal cycler to make many copies of a DNA molecule.

The goals of both RFLP and PCR-based tests are the same: to isolate sequences of DNA at specific locations along the DNA ladder and to take pictures of these DNA sequences that can be identified and compared. But PCR-based tests can be completed in much less time, using samples that contain far less DNA than the samples needed for RFLP tests, at about the same cost. However, the results of PCR-based tests are not as complete and conclusive as the results of RFLP tests. The RFLP results show more matches at more locations on the DNA ladder, producing a more complete version of a DNA fingerprint.

Mullis rightly saw that his discovery had revolutionized molecular biology. "It was a chemical procedure that would make the structures of the molecules of our genes as easy to see as billboards in the desert and as easy to manipulate as Tinkertoys," he said.[10]

In 1993, Mullis won the Nobel Prize for chemistry, the most sought-after award a research scientist can hope for, for the discovery of the PCR technique. The research company he was working for when he made the PCR discovery owned the rights to the technique. After they *patented* PCR, they paid Mullis a $10,000 bonus and sold the patent rights to another research company for $30 million.

Kary Mullis discovered the polymerase chain reaction (PCR) method for the analysis of DNA samples.

Practical Uses

Jeffreys profited more from his discovery than Mullis did from his. He immediately applied for a patent on his RFLP process. An entrepreneur as well as a research scientist, Jeffreys realized that he was onto something that might make him a very wealthy man one day. But first he would have to figure out some practical uses for his new DNA fingerprinting process.

"In theory, we knew it could be used for *forensic* identification and for *paternity testing*," he said. "We could also see the technique working on animals and birds. We could figure out how creatures were related to one another—if you want to understand the natural history of a species, this is basic information. We could also see it being applied to conservation biology. The list of applications seemed endless."[11]

The great expectations of Jeffreys and his research team would come true. Within a very few years, DNA fingerprinting would have an enormously powerful impact on the field of law enforcement, an impact that would continue to grow over time. The discoveries of Jeffreys and Mullis would arm police officers and prosecutors with powerful new weapons for identifying and convicting violent criminals. Within a decade, their discoveries would also begin to have a profound effect on other fields, including medicine, conservation, crop farming, animal breeding, and human history. The impact of DNA fingerprinting was destined to extend far and wide, all around the world and in a very short, very eventful period of time.

Chapter 2

EARLY USES

The First Big Test

How was DNA fingerprinting first used? Alec Jeffreys had a paternity case in mind for the first practical use of his discovery. He believed he could use DNA fingerprinting to prove the identity of a child's father. To find out, Jeffreys tested the DNA of the members of several different families. Just as he had suspected, the results for each family were the same. For each child, half the bands on the X-ray film of the DNA fingerprint belonged to the mother and half to the father.

"You take the child's banding pattern and that of the mother and the alleged father," Jeffreys explained. "The bands on the child's DNA fingerprint that are not from the mother must be inherited from the true father."[1]

In 1985, DNA fingerprinting was first put to the test in what proved to be a landmark immigration case. Why was paternity such an important immigration issue in Britain? Anyone wanting to immigrate there from another country must be a blood relation of a British citizen and must be able to prove it.

The central figure in the case was a boy who had been born in the United States and had then emigrated from there to live in

Ghana with his father. Meanwhile, his mother had immigrated to Britain to become a British citizen. The boy now wished to immigrate to Britain to be with his mother and his three brothers and sisters. But immigration authorities suspected that the boy was not who he said he was. Unless he could prove that he was his mother's son, he would have to leave the country.

To prove that the boy truly was his mother's son, he needed to provide a sample of his father's blood for testing, but his father could not be found. This meant that traditional blood typing could not be used to establish the boy's paternity. The case had dragged on for nearly 2 years when the boy's mother heard about Jeffreys' discovery. She turned to him for help.

Jeffreys jumped at this opportunity to put his discovery to its first big test. He performed a DNA analysis of the family, minus the absent father. The father didn't have to be there, because his DNA was present—in the DNA fingerprints of the other family members.

"Every one of the boy's genetic characteristics could be found in the woman and in the missing father's three other children. It was overwhelming evidence that the boy was a full member of the family," Jeffreys said. "It was a golden moment to see the look on that poor woman's face when she heard that her 2-year nightmare had ended."[2]

Criminal Connection

Jeffreys had no special interest in *forensic science*. He'd never done research on the use of scientific techniques to solve crimes and catch criminals. But it had occurred to him that DNA fingerprinting might one day become a powerful forensic tool. Tests that Jeffreys had run showed that a DNA fingerprint could be obtained from the slightest bit of tissue, even dried specks of 3-year-old blood and semen stains. In fact, virtually any biological evidence, even a single hair, left at the scene of a crime could produce a DNA fingerprint.

Experts could then match this DNA evidence to the person who'd left it behind. And because no two persons share the same DNA fingerprint—with the sole exception of identical twins—the identity of the person who'd left the DNA evidence at the crime scene would be established beyond a reasonable doubt.

But until nearly 2 years after Jeffreys' discovery, DNA fingerprinting was not used to solve crimes. It was Jeffreys himself who became a central figure in the first case in history in which DNA fingerprinting solved a murder.

Rape and Murder

Actually, there were two murders, and both were committed only a few miles from Jeffreys' laboratory in Leicester, England. The first victim was Lynda Mann, a 15-year-old schoolgirl from the nearby village of Narborough. She died on November 1, 1983, after being raped and strangled. Police, who had kept semen stains found on her clothing as evidence, had not found the killer.

The authorities still had no likely suspects in the Mann case when, nearly 3 years later, another young girl was killed. The body of Dawn Ashworth, also 15, was found on July 31, 1986, in the nearby village of Enderby, less than 1 mile (1.6 kilometers) from the site where Mann's body had been found. Like Mann, Ashworth had been raped and strangled, and police found semen stains on her clothing too.

The focus of the investigation was a nearby psychiatric hospital. The police learned that a kitchen worker at the hospital had been seen on the night of the crime near where Ashworth's body was found.

The police took the kitchen worker, who was 17 and had a record of minor sex offenses, in for questioning. Certain that they had the killer, they continued the questioning through the night and morning and into the next afternoon. During those hours of intense questioning, the young man changed his story several times, until finally he admitted that yes, he had seen Ashworth that night. But no, he still insisted, he hadn't killed the girl—he hadn't even so much as talked to her.

The police still believed they had found their killer, but they had to find a way to make him confess. Maybe if they made his crime seem less serious than it really was, they could get him to confess. Police interrogation training manuals refer to this as the "minimization strategy." Perhaps, they suggested, he hadn't really meant to kill Ashworth. Perhaps he'd just wanted to talk to her, and things had gotten out of hand somehow. He hadn't really meant to hurt her at all. The killing had been accidental, hadn't it?

The strategy worked. Yes, the young man finally admitted, he had killed the girl. And he proceeded to describe in detail how he'd raped and strangled Ashworth.

Now for the Lynda Mann murder. The police were certain that the same man had committed both murders, and that man had to be the one who'd confessed to strangling Dawn Ashworth. But this time the young man would not cooperate. He flatly refused to admit that he had anything to do with the 1983 killing of Mann, and no amount of police questioning could get him to change his mind.

The police were desperate now. They had read about Jeffreys' work with DNA in the newspapers. "That DNA bloke [fellow]," they called him. They knew about his startling claims that he could use DNA fingerprinting to establish positive identity from as little as a single speck of human tissue. But the police were highly skeptical of using technical scientific methods to solve crimes. The chief investigator on the case, Derek Pearce, said, "I'd like to see one of these scientists startle me someday."[3]

Pearce didn't know it yet, but he was going to be extremely startled. Pearce had the detective inspector from Leicestershire Constabulary send evidence from the Mann and Ashworth cases for analysis to "that DNA bloke."

A Killer's Signature

The police sent Jeffreys three pieces of evidence: specks of the semen stains from each girl's clothing, along with a blood sample from the confessed murderer. Alec Jeffreys subjected each piece of evidence to his RFLP analysis. He isolated DNA molecules from the semen samples and then compared them with the DNA patterns in the blood of the man who had confessed to the Ashworth murder. The tests took weeks.

Finally, Chief Superintendent David Baker got the phone call he'd been anxiously awaiting. First, Jeffreys said, he had some bad news for the chief superintendent. "Not only is your man innocent in the Mann case, he isn't even the man who killed Dawn Ashworth." Then came the good news. "You only have to catch one killer. The same man murdered both girls," Jeffreys said. The semen stains from the two murdered girls' clothing had produced the same DNA fingerprint. "We have here the signature of the real murderer."[4]

That DNA fingerprint was different from the one Jeffreys had obtained from the suspect's blood sample. All those hours of questioning had finally intimidated the weak-willed young man into making a false confession. But his DNA could not be intimidated into implicating him. The 17-year-old kitchen worker became the first falsely accused man to be freed as a result of DNA fingerprinting evidence. On November 21, 1986, he was released from custody. Alec Jeffreys said, "If we hadn't developed the technology, I'm confident he would have been jailed for life."[5]

But what about the real killer? As Jeffreys said, they now had his "signature," a DNA fingerprint that could belong to no one else but the man who had killed Lynda Mann and Dawn Ashworth.

If the killer had left behind a digital fingerprint, it could have been checked against the ones on record. The police had thousands of digital fingerprints on file. Police have been keeping records of digital fingerprints since the early part of the twentieth century. But they had never used DNA fingerprinting before, so they had no DNA fingerprint records. Somehow they would have to get hold of the DNA fingerprints of possible suspects to compare with those of the killer's.

But how? Virtually every one of the thousands of young men in the area, with the exception of the kitchen worker, was a potential suspect. Chief Superintendent David Baker had an idea. If there were no records, he reasoned, then the police would have to go out and get them, with the help of Alec Jeffreys. "We're going to try something that's never been done," he announced.[6] And with that announcement, the first DNA-based manhunt officially began.

The 4,583rd Man

Officials planned to carry out their search in the villages of Narborough and Enderby, where the bodies had been found, and the neighboring village of Littlethorpe. Every male between the ages of 17 and 34 would be asked to submit blood and saliva samples for Jeffreys to test.

The key word was "asked." The police had no legal right to demand cooperation of anyone who was not under direct suspicion. But these men would be under great social pressure to cooperate. Supposing the killer struck again? The tests were designed to protect the sisters and daughters of these men from the threat of rape and murder. How could you not cooperate?

Unless, of course, you were the killer himself. The police didn't really expect the killer of Lynda Mann and Dawn Ashworth to step forward and volunteer his blood and saliva for Jeffreys to test. But by bringing so much pressure to bear on the entire community, they might get lucky.

The tests began in January 1987. The police were fanatically thorough. Blooding stations, as they were called, were set up in each village. Teams of mobile technicians called "bloodletters" worked in outlying areas, driving as many as 500 miles (800

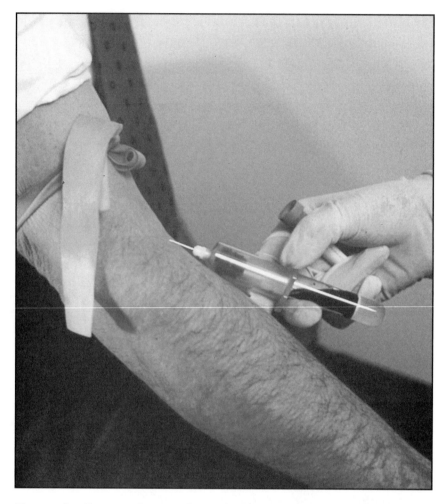

To catch the murderer of Lynda Mann and Dawn Ashworth, authorities asked every man between the ages of 17 and 34 to submit blood and saliva samples for DNA testing.

kilometers) in a single day to collect samples. They were surprised to find that so many men were so afraid of needles. One man said that he'd rather have the doctor punch him in the mouth than prick him with a needle. Another man insisted that the doctor put the needle away and cut his finger with a knife instead. Some men actually fainted at the mere sight of the needle.

But everyone cooperated—everyone but the killer himself. By late July 1987, the police had collected blood and saliva samples from 4,582 men. Jeffreys had tested them all, and none matched the killer's DNA fingerprint. It looked like all those long, hard months of painstaking work had been for nothing.

Then, what the police had been hoping would happen finally happened, though they didn't find out about it until weeks afterward. It happened on August 1 in a Leicester tavern, where four workers from a nearby bakery had come to have drinks and chat. When the talk turned to the DNA manhunt, one of the men at the table, Ian Kelly, admitted that he'd done something he probably shouldn't have. Colin Pitchfork, who also worked at the bakery, had bullied the timid Kelly into going to the police, claiming that he was Pitchfork and taking the blood test in Pitchfork's place, using a faked passport.

One of the women at the table overheard Kelly's remarks. She was upset and confused. What should she do? She didn't like the 27-year-old Colin Pitchfork. None of the women at the bakery did. He had a nasty habit of harassing female employees. But she didn't want to be a snitch, and she didn't want to get poor Ian Kelly into trouble. Finally, after six weeks of wrestling with her conscience, she decided to call the police and report what she had heard that night in August.

The police arrested Colin Pitchfork at his Littlethorpe home on September 19, and they immediately sent samples of his blood and saliva to Jeffreys. Pitchfork was the 4,583rd man to be tested in the great DNA manhunt—and the last. His DNA fingerprint proved to be a perfect match for the killer's. On January 22, 1988, Pitchfork confessed to the murders of Lynda Mann and Dawn Ashworth, and he received two life sentences.

With Pitchfork's confession, DNA fingerprinting had played an instrumental role in two critical events. Without DNA fingerprinting, an innocent man would have gone to prison for life and a killer would have gone free.

Colin Pitchfork was convicted of the murders of Lynda Mann and Dawn Ashworth on the basis of DNA fingerprinting evidence.

Reaction to Jeffreys' triumph was immediate and worldwide. Jeffreys' new technique of DNA fingerprinting was widely acknowledged as the most significant breakthrough in forensic science since the discovery of digital fingerprints.

Reckless Enthusiasm

Jeffreys' astonishing work in solving the Mann and Ashworth murders became known all over the world. In those early years, most people associated DNA fingerprinting exclusively with forensic science. They hailed it as a powerful tool that would revolutionize the entire criminal justice system. One judge called it "the single greatest advance in the search for truth since the advent of *cross-examination*."[7]

In response to all this attention, DNA fingerprinting laboratories sprang up to serve the legal community. The first was Cellmark Diagnostics, which opened a laboratory in 1987 in Germantown, Maryland, using Jeffreys' RFLP technique. They trademarked the name "DNA Fingerprint" to identify the technique. Cellmark went to great lengths to publicize its services. One of its magazine advertisements featured a drawing of a pair of handcuffs in the distinctive double-stranded pattern characteristic of DNA.

The first actual use of DNA evidence to catch a criminal in the United States came in the trial of Tommy Lee Andrews, an accused rapist, that same year. Scientists from Lifecodes laboratories of Valhalla, New York, a rival of Cellmark, testified that semen found on the victim matched Andrews' DNA fingerprint. Andrews was found guilty and sentenced to 22 years in prison.

The Andrews case, which was reported on television and in newspapers nationwide, marked the beginning of a media blitz. Suddenly DNA fingerprinting evidence was showing up in courts everywhere. And wherever this evidence was presented, the conclusions based on it went virtually unchallenged. Defense attorneys faced with DNA fingerprinting evidence against their clients were caught off guard. They had no idea how to begin to counter this complex and highly technical evidence. One defense attorney put it this way: "In rape cases, when the semen has been matched with the defendant's and the chance that it came from another person is 33 billion to 1, you don't need a jury."

Judges and juries also seemed to accept the results without challenge, although they didn't really understand the scientific processes used to obtain this evidence. As one juror put it, "You can't argue with science."[8]

Never before in the history of law enforcement had a new technique for analysis of physical evidence been adopted so suddenly and so unreservedly. It seemed as if DNA fingerprinting were foolproof. In their reckless enthusiasm, people were ignoring the irrefutable fact that any system run by humans for humans is always subject to human error. It wouldn't be long before these errors would be noticed. The public's unquestioning attitude toward DNA fingerprinting was about to undergo a radical change.

Chapter 3

DNA FINGERPRINTING ON TRIAL

DNA testing laboratories, such as Cellmark and Lifecodes, reaped huge benefits from the sudden need for DNA fingerprinting evidence. These private companies were at the forefront of a new and highly profitable industry that they both wanted to dominate.

This fierce competition led to problems. In their rush to be first and best, these rival laboratories ignored the inescapable fact that standardization is essential in evidence testing. Courts demand that all laboratories perform their evidence testing under the same set of exacting standards. Otherwise, DNA fingerprinting tests do not hold up in court.

But setting standards means sharing information, and these rival laboratories were determined to keep their methods secret. They were competing to see who could make the biggest profit, so instead of cooperating, they fought. They challenged one another over patents and licensing issues. They raced to see who could get their own secret, exclusive methods into the courtroom first, most often, and most effectively.

Is This Science?

Because the technologies and methods these companies used to produce DNA fingerprinting evidence remained such closely guarded secrets, independent sources could not evaluate them. Things were not supposed to work this way in the scientific community. Before a new scientific method could be widely used, it was supposed to be described in detail in a scientific journal. Then other scientists, working independently, could review and evaluate the method. As part of their review, they would follow the same steps to see whether they obtained the same results.

However, these rival DNA fingerprinting laboratories never allowed independent sources to inspect their facilities for review and evaluation. No one looked over their shoulder and criticized their work. No one except the scientists doing the actual laboratory testing knew for sure exactly how or under what conditions DNA evidence was obtained.

As a result, the rival companies decided they didn't have to invest the time and money to put systems in place to ensure quality control. They became arrogant about their work. They became unprofessional and sloppy. One geneticist put it this way: "Clinical laboratories have to meet higher requirements to be allowed to diagnose a case of strep throat than a forensic laboratory has to meet to put a defendant on death row."[1]

All this came to light one day in New York City in 1989. Before that day, DNA evidence in nearly 100 cases had been presented in U.S. courtrooms without serious challenge. Then came *People v. Castro.*

The First Challenge: *People v. Castro*

On February 5, 1987, Jeffrey Otero walked into his Bronx apartment and discovered the bodies of his wife and daughter—they had been stabbed to death. A detective investigating the double murder noticed what he thought might be a dried bloodstain on the wristwatch of a neighbor, Jose Castro. This dried bloodstain and the methods used to analyze it led to the first major court challenge to DNA fingerprinting evidence in history—the case known as *People v. Castro.*

Castro became the prime suspect in the double murder of Otero's wife and daughter. The dried blood from his watchband was sent to Lifecodes for analysis, along with samples of the suspect's blood and the blood of the two victims. After analyzing the blood samples, Lifecodes scientists came to the conclusion that the dried blood on Castro's watchband produced a DNA fingerprint identical to that of Otero's murdered wife. If no further evidence were presented to refute this powerful DNA fingerprinting evidence, Castro would, in all likelihood, be found guilty of murder.

The lawyers on Castro's defense team, Barry Scheck and Peter Neufeld, decided to do what very few defense lawyers had done until now. They would challenge the DNA evidence in an effort to have it excluded from testimony. This challenge led to what was known as a Frye hearing. According to the Frye standard, which was based on a 1923 District of Columbia court decision, scientific evidence presented in a court of law must meet three important standards:

- Any evidence of a technical, scientific nature must be based on a valid theory.
- To obtain this evidence, this theory must be applied through a valid technique.
- In the obtaining of this evidence, this valid technique must be properly carried out.

The key word "valid" meant that the scientific technique in question had to be well established and accepted by scientists in that particular field. The Castro defense team was calling into question the basic nature of DNA evidence. DNA fingerprinting itself was being put on trial.

Scheck and Neufeld thought they had a strong point. They knew that there had been a rush to introduce DNA fingerprinting evidence into the U.S. judicial system. In this rush, independent scientists had never evaluated the scientific techniques used to obtain this evidence. Scheck and Neufeld suspected that Lifecodes had never established a common set of standards for analyzing the evidence. If so, they reasoned, the methods used to analyze the bloodstain on their client's watchband would not meet the Frye standard of general acceptance. The judge would then have to exclude the DNA fingerprinting evidence, and their client would go free.

Two Glaring Errors

Both sides, prosecution and defense, brought expert witnesses to testify at the Frye hearing. These witnesses were scientists who were experts in the field of DNA fingerprinting. After a careful examination of the evidence, both sides found something fundamentally wrong.

Lifecodes had made two glaring errors with the Castro evidence. First, the Lifecodes scientists who ran the tests had done a sloppy job of obtaining the DNA fingerprints. Two extra bands had appeared in the print of Otero's slain wife, bands that were not present in the print obtained from the watchband blood. In other words, though Lifecodes said the two DNA fingerprints matched, they actually did not match.

Lifecodes insisted that these two extra DNA bands were irrelevant. They were simply the result of bacterial contamination and had nothing whatever to do with the actual composition of the DNA fingerprint of the murdered woman. Defense attorneys countered that Lifecodes had discounted those extra bands because those bands went against the conclusion that this DNA fingerprint matched the one on the watchband.

To prove that the prints really did match, Lifecodes could have simply performed another test under more exacting conditions, where this bacterial contamination could not have occurred. But the scientists at Lifecodes elected to let the results stand as they were.

Lifecodes' second fundamental error came in the way they interpreted their results. Unlike a digital fingerprint, which presents a complete picture of all the ridges and valleys on the finger or thumb, a DNA fingerprint presents only a partial picture, revealing the DNA sequence at a few locations along the long, winding DNA ladder of the genome. No two people have the same genome, but the sequence at certain locations along the DNA ladder in two people could be identical.

So in their report to the court, Lifecodes had to answer this question: What is the likelihood that the blood on Castro's watchband came not from the murdered woman but from someone else who happened to have the same DNA sequence—at least at a few of the same locations that Lifecodes had tested?

The chance of this actually happening, while very small, is slightly more likely with people of the same racial background. The victims and suspect in the Castro case were all Hispanic Americans so, to calculate the odds, Lifecodes used a database of Hispanic Americans. This database calculated the frequency with which each DNA variation at each tested location occurred in that particular population group. By multiplying these frequencies, Lifecodes arrived at a figure for the complete DNA profile. They concluded that the chance of anyone else in that database having the same DNA sequence at each of the locations Lifecodes had tested was 1 in 189,200,000.

The scientists acting as expert witnesses for the defense at the Frye hearing disagreed with the interpretation made by Lifecodes. They said that Lifecodes had exaggerated the statistics. Actually, the chance of someone else in the Hispanic population sharing the same genetic sequence at each of the tested locations, while still small, was several thousand percent greater than Lifecodes had stated.

On May 11, 1989, the scientists acting as expert witnesses for both the defense and the prosecution issued a joint statement saying that the DNA evidence as presented by Lifecodes was not scientifically reliable. "If these data were submitted to a peer-reviewed journal in support of a conclusion, they would not be accepted. Further experimentation would be required."[2] (A peer-reviewed journal is a magazine in which scientists in a certain field give their opinions on the reliability of other scientists' work.)

In other words, the DNA evidence as presented by Lifecodes did not meet the Frye standard of general acceptance, and so should be excluded from the trial. On August 14, 1989, Acting Justice Gerald Sheindlin of the State Supreme Court agreed. "The testing laboratory failed in several major aspects to use the generally accepted scientific techniques and experiments for obtaining reliable results, within a reasonable degree of scientific certainty."[3] The Lifecodes evidence would be excluded. The prosecution's case against Castro rested almost entirely on that DNA evidence. With Sheindlin's ruling, their case fell apart.

Doubts and Concerns

People v. Castro didn't end there. Jose Castro later confessed to the murders of Otero's wife and daughter and admitted that the blood on his watchband had in fact come from the victim. Although Lifecodes had sloppily presented and inaccurately interpreted the DNA fingerprinting evidence, it was proved true in the end. And Justice Sheindlin ruled that while the procedures in this particular DNA analysis made the evidence unreliable, this did not mean that DNA typing techniques themselves were not reliable. He saw no reason why DNA evidence in general should not continue to be admissible in a court of law.

In the flurry of publicity about DNA evidence that followed, Castro's confession and Sheindlin's ruling were virtually ignored. Doubts had surfaced and were not about to go away. DNA evidence would no longer be accepted without question. People began expressing the same sorts of doubts and concerns that accompany any new field of technical scientific evidence.

These doubts and concerns were not unreasonable. There were serious built-in problems with DNA evidence. For one thing, this highly technical evidence could be quite bewildering to nonscientists. There was always the danger that jurors would be intimidated in the face of such complex technical information. Defense attorneys were concerned that prosecutors would use DNA evidence to overwhelm jurors and persuade them to overlook any other evidence.

Even the defense attorneys themselves could be overwhelmed. Neufeld expressed it this way:

> In the first two dozen cases where DNA evidence was introduced, the opposing attorney did not even challenge the evidence. They felt scientifically illiterate and unable to even perceive of questions. No adverse experts were even retained by the counsel. Everyone just sort of lay down and died.[4]

The Anti-DNA Crusade

After the Castro case, Castro's defense team of Scheck and Neufeld seized on these doubts and concerns to launch an all-out crusade against DNA evidence. It was a crusade that they would continue for years to come. Scheck and Neufeld disagreed strongly with Justice Sheindlin. They insisted that the results of the Castro case clearly demonstrated that DNA evidence was not reliable and should not be allowed in a court of law.

In 1989, as part of their crusade, Scheck and Neufeld launched a DNA Task Force for the National Association of Criminal Defense Lawyers (NACDL). Other defense lawyers joined them. Not surprisingly, a high official at Lifecodes countered DNA critics by writing, "They call for a moratorium on DNA evidence. But isn't that simply a desperate attempt to neutralize a technology they can't defeat in court?"[5]

By now the Federal Bureau of Investigation (FBI) had entered the picture as well. This federal law-enforcement agency had been interested in DNA evidence testing ever since Alec Jeffreys' discovery of DNA fingerprinting in 1984. In collaboration with the National Institutes of Health, the FBI had been researching DNA evidence techniques. In late 1988, the FBI set up its own DNA evidence laboratory at its Washington, D.C., headquarters on Pennsylvania Avenue. The FBI made DNA testing available at no charge to law-enforcement authorities nationwide.

At the same time, the Royal Canadian Mounted Police (RCMP), the national law-enforcement agency in Canada, began its own DNA testing. The FBI and the RCMP performed a service that the unruly DNA evidence industry badly needed. They cooperated to set up detailed standards for DNA testing. Unlike Lifecodes and Cellmark, these two law-enforcement agencies were not in competition. With no profit motive at stake, they had no reason to keep their technologies and methods secret from each another. Instead, they actively pooled their knowledge to bring standardization to an industry very much in need of it.

However, Scheck and Neufeld were not impressed, and they pushed forward with their anti-DNA crusade. Their early efforts had little if any effect on the legal system itself. DNA evidence continued to be accepted in courts of law.

But in the court of public opinion, it was a different story. Like Scheck and Neufeld, the news media seized on these newfound doubts and concerns about DNA evidence. Before *People v. Castro,* the press had printed articles about DNA evidence that were nearly all positive. Now the articles had turned negative. One of the most critical appeared on January 20, 1990, on the front page of the *New York Times*. "Some Scientists Doubt the Value of 'Genetic Fingerprint' Evidence," the headline proclaimed.

The *Times* headline was incorrect, and the article was riddled with misinformation and misstatements. The article claimed that several leading *molecular biologists* had expressed grave doubts about the validity of DNA testing.

Supposedly, these scientists, who study the structure and function of molecules, believed that DNA analysis was "too unreliable to be used in court," and that it "cannot be counted on to decide with virtual certainty whether a person is guilty of a crime" because "DNA fingerprints can stretch and shift, like a design printed on rubber, making them difficult, if not impossible, to interpret. They say that even without these shifts, DNA patterns can be almost impossible to compare." The article also alleged that these scientists had so little confidence in DNA testing that "they would not allow their DNA fingerprints to be taken if they were innocent suspects in a criminal case."[6]

The article would not have caused such a stir if it had appeared in any other publication. But the *New York Times* is one of the most respected newspapers in the nation, and this time it had the facts wrong. The molecular biologists named in the article were outraged. Four of them drafted an immediate letter of correction. Their letter to the *Times* was clear and unambiguous. There is "excellent agreement among scientists that the validity of the DNA identification method is widely accepted," they wrote.[7]

For reasons the *New York Times* never explained, it chose not to publish this letter of correction. In the wake of the *Times* article, newspapers all over the nation ran stories questioning the use of DNA as evidence. Then came an event that sparked yet another flurry of misinterpretations about DNA testing.

More Controversy: The National Research Council Report

In 1990, the National Research Council (NRC), which is part of the National Academy of Sciences, undertook a federally funded study of DNA testing. A panel of molecular biologists headed the study. Their goal was to clear up the controversy and help the courts decide once and for all whether and under what conditions DNA evidence should be allowed.

The NRC study, *DNA Techniques in Forensic Science,* was two years in the making. Two days before its official release on April 16, 1992, the *New York Times* ran a story predicting what the report would say. "U.S. Panel Seeking Restriction on Use of DNA in Courts, Judges Are Asked to Bar Genetic 'Fingerprinting' Until Basis in Science Is Stronger" the headline proclaimed. This story, written by the same science reporter who had written the earlier article, claimed the NRC panel would recommend that courts stop using DNA fingerprinting evidence "until laboratory standards have been tightened and the technique has been established on a stronger scientific basis."[8]

In their haste to beat other news sources to the punch, the *New York Times* once again had the facts wrong. Actually, the panel would recommend that DNA evidence continue to be used in the courts without interruption. The chairperson of the report's panel was Victor McKusick, a geneticist at Johns Hopkins University. McKusick met in person with reporters to set the record straight. The next day the *Times* printed a front-page retraction headlined "Times Account in Error." The retraction quoted McKusick as saying, "We think that DNA can be used in court without interruption."[9]

McKusick and the other members of the panel hoped that the long-awaited 185-page report would help end the controversy about the admissibility of DNA evidence in court. But the report was long, rambling, and unclear in places. Scientists and lawyers alike seriously criticized the positions the panel took on calculating the probability of a DNA fingerprinting match. Rather than end the controversy, the 1992 NRC report had the opposite effect. For years after its issue, defense attorneys used it to help them fight the admissibility of DNA evidence in court.

The Issue of Standards

After two more years of controversy, in criminal courts and in the media, one issue regarding DNA evidence was finally laid to rest. The scientific and law-enforcement communities came to a mutual agreement: DNA fingerprinting should now be regarded as a legitimate form of evidence, fully as admissible in court as digital fingerprinting evidence.

An article published in the October 27, 1994, issue of the influential British journal *Nature* signaled this mutual agreement. The two authors of the article were Bruce Budowle, a chief architect of the FBI's DNA typing program, and Eric Lander, a prominent geneticist from the Massachusetts Institute of Technology and a harsh critic of DNA evidence. The two men agreed that DNA fingerprinting was probably the most powerful tool ever devised for identifying criminals.

"The DNA fingerprinting wars are over," Budowle and Lander declared. "The scientific debates served a salutary purpose: standards were professionalized and research stimulated. But now it is time to move on." There was no scientific reason to doubt the accuracy of forensic DNA typing results, they wrote, "providing that the testing laboratory and the specific tests are on a par with currently practiced standards in the field."[10]

This last issue of standards would continue to be controversial. If DNA fingerprinting tests were not conducted according to rigorous, painstaking procedures, the DNA samples could easily become contaminated. Lander put it this way: "If I sneeze on something, my DNA is there, too. And so there is tremendous need to avoid contamination."[11]

Lander was referring to the standards that DNA laboratories used in analyzing tissue samples. The FBI and RCMP had gone a long way toward helping to standardize laboratory practices in DNA testing and thus improving the reliability of results. But that nagging problem that no advance in technology could make go away—human error—would continue to plague the credibility of DNA evidence. The outcome of one notoriously famous case in particular would hinge on human error in the handling of DNA evidence. This trial was destined to become known as "the trial of the century."

O.J. Simpson, the former football player and sportscaster, tries on one of the leather gloves that prosecutors said he was wearing the night he supposedly murdered Nicole Brown and Ronald Goldman in 1994. He was later acquitted of the crime.

The Trial of the Century

The question facing the jury sounded like a simple one. Did O.J. Simpson—a former professional football star, sportscaster, actor, and TV advertising spokesman—kill his former wife, Nicole Brown, and her friend, Ronald Goldman, outside Brown's luxury southern California townhouse on the night of June 12, 1994?

The question sounded simple enough, but getting the answer would be anything but simple. Never before had anyone so famous and so well-liked by so many people been accused of such a savage crime. Simpson's ex-wife's throat had been slit and her friend had been knifed to death. Millions of dollars would be spent by both sides before the trial was over. More than 100 witnesses would be called, more than 1,000 exhibits of evidence would be presented, and nearly 9 months would pass before the question would be answered. And the outcome would hinge largely on the handling of DNA fingerprinting evidence obtained from blood found at the scene of the crime and on the clothing, driveway, and car of O.J. Simpson.

The Prosecution: DNA Fingerprinting Evidence

The prosecution's case in the Simpson trial was based largely on the following DNA evidence:

- A glove found between the bodies stained with blood that gave a DNA match for Simpson, Goldman, and Brown
- Three bloodstains found on the back gate of the crime scene that gave a DNA match for Simpson
- Five drops of blood leading away from the crime scene that gave a DNA match for Simpson
- A speck of blood on Simpson's Ford Bronco that gave a DNA match for Simpson, Goldman, and Brown
- A pair of socks found on Simpson's bedroom floor stained with blood that gave a DNA match for Simpson and Brown

Juries tend to believe DNA evidence when it is properly presented. In this case, if members of the jury had accepted the DNA fingerprinting evidence as true and authentic, they would almost certainly have convicted Simpson.

But as *People v. Castro* proved, the mere existence of DNA evidence does not always lead to conviction. Equally important is the manner in which that DNA evidence was collected and tested. And that was where the Simpson defense team concentrated their attack.

The Defense: Alleged Conspiracy

The defense team's point of attack was not the DNA test results themselves. Simpson's lawyers conceded that the RFLP and PCR testing, performed by teams of scientists at Cellmark laboratories and the Department of Justice, was accurate. They agreed that the blood these laboratories tested had come from their client, O.J. Simpson.

However, Simpson's lawyers contended, the blood evidence was suspect. First, members of the Los Angeles Police Department (LAPD) had badly mishandled it. In fact, the lawyers claimed, the mishandling was so bad that it looked as if their client was the victim of a conspiracy. Simpson's lawyers alleged that certain members of the LAPD hated their client so much that they had deliberately rigged the evidence to make Simpson appear to be guilty.

The defense lawyers had a point. The LAPD had indeed done a sloppy job of evidence collection. Police mistakes included sending a trainee instead of an experienced professional to collect blood samples from the scene of this very high-profile crime. The young woman assigned to the job had never even collected blood from a crime scene before. Also, bloodstain evidence from the crime scene, stored in a plastic bag, remained in a truck for several hours on a hot day, creating conditions that could very likely damage the DNA in the bloodstain. The defense argued that these facts alone proved that the LAPD was incompetent to handle scientific evidence.

The police made another, more serious mistake after blood was drawn from Simpson. An LAPD detective was supposed to turn the Simpson blood sample in for testing. But instead of bringing the vial of blood straight to the police department, he carried it around with him in an unsealed envelope for 3 hours, during which time he stopped to have a cup of coffee. Only then did he bring it in for testing. Later, records revealed that a significant portion of this blood was missing. The police could not account for it.

Simpson's defense team argued that these facts pointed to something far more serious than mere incompetence. The missing Simpson blood, they maintained, was evidence of a conspiracy on the part of certain members of the LAPD to frame their client. The lawyers claimed that the police had used the missing Simpson blood to plant DNA evidence at the scene of the crime and on Simpson's clothing, car, and driveway.

Actually, Simpson's blood had been drawn at 3:30 p.m. on June 13, several hours after the police had already collected most of the bloodstain evidence and turned it in for testing. Without a sample of Simpson's blood at their disposal, how could the police have planted it as evidence? It was not physically possible.

However, it turned out that not all of the bloodstain evidence was collected before Simpson's sample was drawn. The police had collected blood from stains found on Simpson's socks and on the back gate at Brown's townhouse several weeks later. So it *was* physically possible that the police could have used the missing Simpson blood to plant the stains on Brown's gate and Simpson's socks.

But why would they do such a terrible thing? What motive could the police have for conspiring to frame O.J. Simpson? The motive Simpson's lawyers offered was based on race. Simpson was African-American. An LAPD detective named Mark Fuhrman, who was closely involved in the investigation, was a white man who had made a number of racial slurs against African-Americans in the past. Apart from this lone fact, Simpson's lawyers offered the jury no clear reason why the LAPD would want to frame their client, much less any proof.

But the defense in a criminal trial does not have to prove anything. The defense does not need to convince a jury of their client's innocence. The burden of proof rests entirely with the opposing side. To win its case, the prosecution must prove guilt beyond a reasonable doubt, while the defense needs only to raise reasonable doubts in the minds of jurors in regard to the

prosecution's evidence. To do this, all the defense has to do is offer the jury reasonable alternative explanations for each piece of evidence against their client. If jurors are left with reasonable doubts at the end of the trial, they are duty-bound to enter a verdict of not guilty.

By focusing on the sloppy evidence collection by the LAPD and the missing sample of Simpson's blood, Simpson's defense lawyers succeeded in raising doubts about the DNA evidence. An expert witness on DNA who took the stand for the defense contributed to these doubts. Dr. John Gerdes, director of a DNA lab in Denver, Colorado, testified that in his opinion, the LAPD Crime Lab had a serious problem with contamination of evidence. Gerdes' testimony served to support the defense contention that even if members of the LAPD were not out to frame Simpson, they were not competent to deal with the DNA evidence being used to convict him.

Reasonable Doubt

Would the defense's allegations of incompetence and conspiracy on the part of the LAPD win out over the seemingly overwhelming DNA fingerprinting evidence presented by the prosecution? The whole world, it seemed, was waiting to find out. This is how one newspaper described the scene in downtown Los Angeles on the morning of October 1, 1995:

> In the hours before the verdict was announced, news helicopters swarmed over the courthouse, police squad cars cruised downtown streets and barricades blocked traffic in front of the Criminal Courts Building. A swelling crowd was moved out of the area in a police sweep.[12]

After listening to 9 months' worth of testimony, the jury deliberated for less than 5 hours before reaching their verdict. Two members of the 12-person jury voted guilty at first. But after further discussion, they changed their vote, and the jury was united in a verdict of not guilty. O.J. Simpson was a free man.

One of the jurors who had changed her vote later explained that while she felt that Simpson may have been guilty, she didn't think the evidence proved it. Referring to the bloody glove found between the slain bodies of Brown and Goldman, she stated, "I thought it was possible it was planted. And most of the evidence was DNA evidence, and that's what was so shaky."[13]

The key word in the juror's statement is "possible." It signals the reasonable doubt that Simpson's defense team was after. The defense had also cited a 1987 incident in which Cellmark, one of the laboratories that did the Simpson DNA testing, had made an error in reporting DNA fingerprinting evidence in another case. Even though the defense did not directly dispute the Simpson DNA testing, they managed to raise enough doubts about the whole DNA testing procedure, beginning with the collection of the DNA evidence at the crime scene, to win their case.

The Simpson verdict gave new ammunition to the opponents of DNA fingerprinting. The success of Simpson's defense team meant that other defense attorneys would use the Simpson case as a model in cases to come. They would no longer be intimidated by DNA test results that pointed toward their client's guilt. They too would mount aggressive challenges to DNA evidence, based on possible mishandling by both laboratories and police. The controversy surrounding DNA testing was not over yet.

Chapter 4

USE AND MISUSE

To win their case, O.J. Simpson's defense team did all they possibly could to create doubt about the reliability of DNA testing. But even after the stunning not-guilty verdict, even after all the problems with mishandling of evidence by the LAPD, most people involved with the criminal justice system still held DNA fingerprinting evidence in high regard. The law-enforcement community still saw it as the single most important scientific breakthrough in determining guilt or innocence since digital fingerprints. DNA fingerprinting was here to stay.

However, the Simpson case radically altered attitudes toward DNA testing. This complex scientific law-enforcement technique could no longer be left to a few scientific experts to explain to the rest of the law-enforcement community. From now on, lawyers and judges would need to have a clear understanding of DNA testing themselves.

Learning About DNA Fingerprinting

Clearly, many people needed a basic science education in a hurry. Like most people who made their living in professional fields outside of science in the 1990s, the 30,000 judges in the

United States didn't have much in the way of scientific training. And of those who did, few had been schooled in genetics. This would have to change. Here was how a prominent scientist and lawyer, Dr. Franklin Zweig, summed up the need: "Judges can no longer afford to be passive umpires of evidence. They have to be active managers of the reliability of evidence. As gatekeepers [of information], they need to know and understand science."[1]

Every year, an increasing number of court cases involve scientific evidence. If juries with little in the way of scientific background can't understand this evidence, they tend to become confused and give up trying. Then, rather than decide the case on the basis of the scientific evidence, they base their verdict on other less relevant grounds. This phenomenon, known as *jury nullification*, is every judge's nightmare. It means that both judge and jury have lost their hold on the case.

If judges did not grasp what DNA testing was all about, Dr. Zweig said, the phenomenon of jury nullification would become more and more common, and the public would eventually lose confidence in the courts. Something had to be done. Zweig, president of the Einstein Institute for Health and the Courts in Bethesda, Maryland, decided to do something about the problem. He designed a national program to educate state and federal judges in genetics and biology, with an emphasis on DNA testing.

In Zweig's program, judges learned the ABCs of genetics and DNA testing from working scientists. Judges were also schooled in detecting so-called "junk science." When witnesses testifying as scientific experts give testimony using "junk science," they are misusing technical scientific terms and facts.

This occurred during the O.J. Simpson trial when John Gerdes testified as an expert witness for the defense (see Chapter 3). Gerdes told the jury that Simpson's DNA fingerprints, obtained from the bloodstains at the crime scene, could have shown up by accident—as a result of contamination of the LAPD's contamination of evidence. This made it sound as though Simpson's DNA fingerprints had shown up by accident in someone else's blood. A prosecution lawyer made Gerdes admit that his testimony was misleading. Under cross-examination, Gerdes admitted that contamination could not possibly cause one person's DNA fingerprint to show up in a sample of someone else's blood.

Gerdes' initial testimony sounded reliable enough to someone unschooled in science. The judge in the Simpson case did not question it. If the prosecution lawyer who cross-examined him had not been schooled in DNA testing, Gerdes's misleading testimony would have been accepted as valid. The Simpson case vividly demonstrated that in order to get at the truth in a case involving DNA testing, lawyers, judges, and juries must clearly understand what DNA fingerprints are and how they are obtained.

DNA Testing Simplified

How could nonscientists understand the complex nature of DNA fingerprinting evidence? Education was one answer—to understand a complex technique, you need to study it. Another answer was to simplify the technique itself—make it easier to understand. And ever since 1984, when Alec Jeffreys and Kary Mullis discovered the RFLP and PCR techniques, the technology of DNA fingerprinting had been becoming simpler and more effective.

How much simpler? One big difference lay in the methods of interpreting data. In *People v. Castro,* the judge excluded the DNA evidence from consideration because Lifecodes had overestimated the mathematical probability of one region of a suspect's DNA fingerprint matching anyone else's on the planet, though the odds were still vast.

That was in 1989. At that time, scientists hadn't had access to enough data to be comfortable with estimating the frequencies of DNA fingerprint patterns occurring in different people. The 1992 NRC report noted this fact.

In May 1996, by the time the NRC issued its second report on the state of DNA testing, the situation had changed. For one thing, more data were available. Scientists had analyzed and classified vast numbers of DNA fingerprint patterns. For another, DNA fingerprinting techniques had improved. Scientists could now obtain more complete DNA fingerprints by sampling more sites along the DNA ladder in less time. The 1996 NRC report announced that the RFLP and PCR-based methods for obtaining DNA fingerprints and the methods for estimating their frequencies were now advanced enough that properly collected and analyzed DNA data should be accepted.

The next year, in November 1997, the FBI said much the same thing. Old DNA fingerprinting technologies, they said, had offered a one-in-thousands chance that someone besides the suspect had the same DNA fingerprint. Current technologies, they announced, had changed the mathematical probability to 1 in 260 billion—on a planet of some 6 billion people. From now on, FBI experts testifying in criminal trials would be able to state with complete confidence that a particular DNA fingerprint could come from one person and one person only.

The Innocence Project

Not even Barry Scheck and Peter Neufeld, the defense lawyers in *People v. Castro,* disagreed. Their anti-DNA crusade, begun in 1989, ended by 1992. They stopped insisting that DNA evidence was not reliable and should not be allowed in a court of law. In fact, they were now champions of DNA fingerprinting evidence. But being defense lawyers, they used this evidence not to send criminals to prison, but to exonerate innocent people, to free people from prison who had been falsely convicted.

Scheck and Neufeld founded the Innocence Project in 1992. It operates out of the Benjamin N. Cardozo School of Law at Yeshiva University in New York City. Law students do most of the work, under the supervision of their professors.

Attorneys Barry Scheck (left) and Peter Neufeld (right) founded the Innocence Project (1992), which works to exonerate convicted persons using new evidence obtained from DNA fingerprinting.

The Innocence Project deals in postconviction exoneration cases. These are cases in which innocent people are freed from prison because new evidence has proven them innocent of the crime for which they have been serving prison time. Where does the new evidence come from? DNA fingerprinting tests provide it.

The process works this way. Inmates write letters to the Innocence Project, stating why they were sent to prison and why they should be freed. If DNA evidence is still on file, and if the inmate's case appears convincing, Innocence Project lawyers work to get the case reopened and the DNA evidence tested. This work is done *pro bono*—free of charge.

Often the case involves sexual assault, where the semen sample of the perpetrator (the person who supposedly committed the crime) is still on file with a city or state crime lab and available for testing. Why wasn't the semen sample tested in the first place? In some instances, the case was tried before the mid-1980s, when courts first began using DNA testing. In other cases, the DNA sample was too small or too degraded to be tested by techniques available at that time.

Advances in DNA fingerprinting technology mean that these tests could now be performed. When the results showed that the inmate's DNA fingerprint did not match the one obtained from the evidence sample, the inmate was set free.

Three Tragic Reasons

Why are innocent people found guilty and sent to prison in the first place? Mistakes are made for three main reasons: false confession, inadequate defense, and mistaken identity.

False confessions may land innocent suspects in prison. These confessions generally come after long hours of intense police interrogation when the suspects believe that they will be found guilty and can only hope that a confession will lighten the sentence. The first wrongly accused suspect saved by DNA fingerprinting evidence was the kitchen worker in the 1987 DNA manhunt, when Alec Jeffreys first used his RFLP technique (see Chapter 2).

Innocent suspects may be found guilty because their lawyer did not prepare an adequate defense. "Nothing convicts an innocent defendant faster than having a bad lawyer," says Scheck.[2] Most of the people who are accused of violent crimes are poor. They don't have the money to hire their own lawyer, so they must settle for one appointed for them by the court. These *public defenders* are often inexperienced and nearly always overburdened. With so many suspects to defend, they don't have the time to prepare a complete defense for their clients.

But a bigger reason than false confessions and an inadequate defense, Scheck said, is mistaken identity. "Mistaken identification is the single greatest cause of the conviction of the innocent. DNA testing is showing us with a great deal of scientific certainty that it's an even greater problem than we suspected."[3] U.S. Supreme Court Justice William Brennan agreed: "The vagaries of eyewitness identification are well known; the annals of criminal law are rife with instances of mistaken identification."[4]

Brennan's remarks appeared in a landmark study by the National Institute of Justice issued in 1996. This study summarized 28 cases in which DNA fingerprinting evidence was instrumental in freeing falsely imprisoned men. By taking a close look at one of these cases, we can see how easily mistaken identity can lead to a miscarriage of justice, and how that miscarriage of justice can then be corrected by DNA fingerprinting evidence.

A False Conviction: *People v. Cotton*

In July 1984, two women were robbed and sexually assaulted in their Burlington, North Carolina, apartments. A month later, Ronald Cotton was arrested for these crimes. He was eventually convicted and sentenced to life plus 54 years in prison.

Cotton was convicted despite two facts. One, family members supported his alibi. Two, one of the victims failed to pick him out of a police lineup. (Later, though, this victim picked Cotton out of another police lineup.)

Cotton's conviction came as a result of two tragic mistakes. The first was mistaken identity on the part of the two victims. The second was a mistake on the part of the judge. Before Cotton's trial, a man already serving time in prison told another inmate that he had committed the crimes with which Cotton had been charged. The judge in the case refused to allow Cotton's lawyer to enter the inmate's confession as evidence.

Another vital piece of evidence was not used in the trial. The real perpetrator of the assaults had left semen stains on the victims' clothing. If experts had tested these stains against Cotton's DNA, Cotton would never have gone to prison. But no tests were performed, because DNA fingerprinting techniques were not used by the courts until years later. Cotton went to prison in 1984.

In 1994, two new lawyers who had taken over Cotton's case filed a motion for DNA testing. The motion was granted, and the results showed no match to Cotton's DNA. But it did show a match

Ronald Cotton (right) was wrongfully convicted of the robbery and rape of two women in 1984. He was freed from prison on the basis of DNA fingerprinting evidence.

to the inmate who, 10 years earlier, had confessed to Cotton's crimes. On June 30, 1995, Cotton was released from prison.

One month later, Cotton received an official pardon from the governor of North Carolina. He had served 10 years in prison for crimes he did not commit. If not for DNA testing, he might have been there for the rest of his life.

Evidence Tragically Withheld

According to the newspaper *USA Today*, in May 2000, the total number of prisoners exonerated by DNA fingerprinting evidence was 64. Lawyers from the Innocence Project had helped free 36 of them. Among the freed people were men who had served up to 16 years behind bars.

While Innocence Project cofounder Scheck believes in the power of DNA evidence, he is quick to point out that this evidence must be properly collected, tested, and reported if it is to be effective. This doesn't always happen, as the O.J. Simpson case dramatically demonstrated. Scheck was a prominent member of Simpson's defense team. "We were able to demonstrate a lot that was wrong with the way the crime lab worked, the medical examiner's office worked, the way the police department functioned," he said.[5]

The case of John Willis makes Scheck's pessimistic view of police crime-lab work believable. Willis spent more than 8 years in the Stateville Correctional Center in Illinois for a sexual assault committed in May 1990. Despite the existence of DNA evidence that proved him innocent, Willis was found guilty. DNA tests of semen stains recovered at the crime scene proved that the assault actually had been committed by Dennis McGruder, a man who looked a great deal like Willis. But instead of reporting this vital fact, the Chicago police lab technician in charge of the test results never revealed this to the court.

Years later, Willis's lawyers managed to get the case reopened when they discovered handwritten notes by the police lab technician who had withheld the test results. The notes contained critical evidence that could have proved Willis innocent at the original trial. A medical examiner who investigated the case concluded that the technician's withholding of evidence could not have been an accident. It must have been deliberate.

Chicago police disagreed. After carrying out their own internal investigation, they concluded that "there was no finding of misconduct on the part of anybody within the Chicago Police Department."[6]

Intentional or not, this tragic mistake caused an innocent man to spend more than 8 years of his life in prison. Scheck believes that thousands of innocent men who are still serving time in prison could be exonerated by DNA evidence, if only that evidence could be tested and evaluated.

Chapter 5

MATCHING THE CRIMINAL WITH THE CRIME

A Huge Backlog

Crime labs do not have the time and money needed to test and evaluate the enormous amount of DNA evidence in existence. A huge backlog of DNA evidence waits to be tested. DNA testing that is properly carried out has a reliability rate of 99.99 percent. That's why more and more prosecutors have come to depend on it to win cases involving physical crime. As a result, crime labs receive a constant flow of requests for DNA testing, far more than they can possibly meet in a timely manner.

DNA evidence takes time to process. As DNA fingerprinting technology continues to improve, testing becomes faster and cheaper. Tests that used to take weeks to complete and cost thousands of dollars now take just hours or minutes to complete and cost just a few dollars. But the volume of DNA tests that need to be performed keeps increasing.

Time continues to be a problem. Crime labs cannot process great quantities of DNA evidence in a rush—nor should they try to do this. The U.S. National Institute of Justice made this clear in their guidelines on certification of DNA labs: "In order for this evidence to stand up in court, legal counsel and judges must be confident, and a jury convinced, that evidentiary samples were collected properly and that a qualified person, using sound procedures, performed the tests and analyzed the results accurately."[1]

Sound procedures and accurate analysis require careful, methodical work by highly qualified individuals. A crime lab cannot hurry its procedures, not even when a batch of new samples arrives. A constant lack of funds prevents city and state crime labs from hiring additional staff and buying more sophisticated equipment to meet the constantly increasing demands. As a result, a backlog of evidence accumulates, with testing delays of weeks, months, and sometimes years.

What This Backlog Means

This delay can mean that a violent suspect who should have been in custody remains free to commit more crimes, while the evidence that could have brought him to justice waits among all the other backlogged cases. Or an innocent person sits in jail while the one piece of evidence that could set him free sits on a shelf in a crime lab waiting to be tested.

Raymond Holder is a case in point. Accused of a violent rape, Holder sat in a Virginia jail for nearly 9 months insisting on his innocence. It took that long for a badly overburdened Virginia state crime lab to test the DNA evidence sample that eventually set Holder free.

But what about the person who *did* commit the rape? While Holder sat in jail and the evidence sat on the shelf, police turned their attention to other matters. Meanwhile, the real criminal remained free to rape again. The Director of the Virginia Division of Forensic Science said, "How many crimes that we took a year to solve could have been solved in a week? And how many further offenses, rapes or murders, were committed by that individual in the meantime?"[2]

Barry Scheck thinks that this dilemma should come as no surprise to anyone involved with the criminal justice system.

"Why is it such a shock that things go wrong? When prosecutors don't have enough resources, when crime labs don't have enough resources? Where calendars are overburdened and judges have difficulties? Why is it such a shock that things go wrong?"[3]

The problems with making DNA evidence available to law-enforcement officials do not begin and end at the police crime lab. Even after the DNA evidence has been analyzed, the result—the DNA fingerprint—must be matched to the person to whom it belongs. And this is not always a simple matter.

Organizing DNA Fingerprinting Evidence

The first DNA manhunt took place in England in 1987 (see Chapter 2). Police had the DNA fingerprint of the killer of two young women, but they had no records of DNA fingerprints to check it against. They had to test 4,583 men before they found a match.

This case had a profound effect on law-enforcement procedures in Britain. It alerted British citizens about the power of DNA finger-printing records. They realized that databanks would allow vast amounts of evidence to be gathered in one place and made ready for comparison. The British government responded by putting a great deal of money into developing a nationwide DNA database. This steady and generous input of funds allows British law-enforcement authorities to eliminate backlogs of DNA information and to add equipment and personnel as needed.

To develop a DNA database, the police collect DNA evidence from crime scenes and from convicted criminals. The resulting DNA fingerprints are stored in computer databases, where they can be quickly and accurately compared. These DNA databases are used in two ways to catch criminals.

1. The criminal leaves behind a DNA sample at the scene of the crime: a hair, skin, blood, semen, or saliva. Samples can come from a variety of sources, including blood left on broken glass during a break-in and bits of an attacker's skin caught beneath a victim's fingernails. The sample is tested, and the resulting

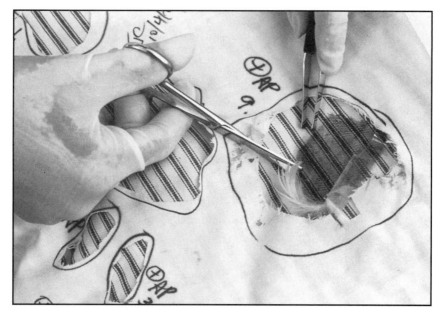

The blood on this pillow from a crime scene can be used to obtain a DNA fingerprint, and it may match the DNA of a previously convicted criminal.

DNA fingerprint is compared against the database. If it matches the DNA of a previously convicted criminal, the criminal is identified. This is known as a *cold hit*.

2. The DNA fingerprint of a newly convicted criminal is entered into the database and checked against DNA fingerprints from other, unsolved cases. If a match is made, then the criminal is charged with those crimes too. This is also known as a cold hit.

In both cases, the criminal is caught by his own genes.

Because so many violent criminals are repeat offenders, a DNA database can be a powerfully effective tool for solving violent crimes. According to a professor of forensic sciences at George Washington University: "Studies have shown that most of the violent crime is committed by a very small number of criminals. If we're able to identify these guys and send them away, or if, instead of convicting the guy for one sexual assault, we get him for 10 and he goes away for the rest of his life, think about the impact that will have on the safety of citizens."[4]

Because these cases involve violent crime, the public notices them. "They're the kinds of cases where people care very dramatically about identifying the people who committed them and getting them off the street," a former New York City prosecutor said. "And DNA databanks make that possible."[5]

In Britain, DNA databases have been well established and well funded since the mid-1980s. But the situation is different in the United States, where development of a nationwide DNA database did not even begin until the 1990s.

A National DNA Database

A 1994 law authorized a nationwide U.S. DNA database, but it wasn't until 1997 that it began to take shape. In December of that year, using FBI software, 8 of the 50 states joined their individual DNA computer databases into one master database, the National DNA Index System (NDIS).

Minutes after the NDIS was put into action, it scored the first cold hit. The database linked a convicted Illinois sex offender with a rape committed in Wisconsin in 1989. According to the FBI, in the first few months of operation of the NDIS, it generated cold hits that solved as many as 300 previously unsolved violent crimes.

By June 1998, all 50 states had passed laws requiring convicted sex offenders to supply DNA samples to be entered in the NDIS database. On November 14, 1998, all 50 states became linked to an FBI computer housing DNA fingerprints obtained from 250,000 convicted criminals and from evidence left at the scenes of 4,600 unsolved violent crimes. The director of the FBI Laboratory announced that the "NDIS allows this exciting technology to reach its full potential in solving violent crimes through nationwide information sharing among the 94 public crime laboratories conducting examinations."[6]

But the database has been slow in reaching its potential. As of May 2000, only 24 states were actively contributing DNA fingerprints to the database on a regular basis, and some 750,000 samples taken from convicts still had not been analyzed. Other states have been lagging behind because of problems with the collection and analysis of DNA.

Civil Justice versus Civil Liberties

No one can say that the NDIS is not effective in bringing violent criminals to justice. From 1992 through April 2000, the FBI made DNA matches in some 851 crimes by using various databases, including NDIS. Nevertheless, NDIS has come under continual fire. The criticism centers on just whose DNA should be tested and entered into the nationwide database.

In February 1998, thousands of Massachusetts prison inmates were ordered to give blood samples for DNA testing and entry into the database. Many of these inmates were not violent criminals. Several of them sued the state. This gathering of DNA samples amounted to illegal search and seizure, they argued in their suit, and illegal search and seizure is outlawed by the U.S. Constitution. A judge agreed and halted the procedure.

An attorney representing the inmates expressed his own outrage at the situation in Massachusetts. "Why not round up all the poor people?" he said sarcastically. "Poor people are more likely to commit a crime, so shouldn't we have their DNA on file too? Of course, there are benefits every time you get a cold hit. There are going to be dramatic success stories. But where does it stop? Why not take DNA samples at birth?"[7]

In an article about this event, a science editor for the *New York Times* added that DNA techniques had become so reliable and so efficient that "some civil libertarians fear it will be expanded from people convicted of crimes to include almost everyone, giving the Government inordinate investigative powers over citizens."[8]

A professor of public policy at the University of Washington echoed the concerns expressed by the *New York Times* editor. The way the situation looked to him, the FBI DNA database "will probably be extended to include everyone, giving elites the power to control 'unruly' citizens."[9]

Finally, Dr. Eric Juengst, a key member of the FBI's DNA Advisory Board, expressed his own concerns. When the FBI originally set up the database, he said, it was their expressed policy that the database would include DNA fingerprints only for the most violent criminals. Expanding the scope of the database to include anyone beyond convicted violent criminals would be a breach of FBI policy, he insisted.

Expand the Database?

Nevertheless, law-enforcement authorities kept pushing for expansion. Authorities in Oregon decided to expand their DNA fingerprinting database. They would include not only offenders convicted of homicide and sexual assault, but those found guilty of burglary and serious assault as well. Oregon State Police insisted that this move was justified. They said that people who commit crimes such as burglary and assault often go on to commit more serious violent crimes, including rape. Florida law-enforcement officials agreed. They found that more than 50 percent of the people they were matching to sex crimes or murders through their DNA database had already committed burglary or aggravated assault.

These were small steps, though, compared to the steps that law-enforcement authorities in other states were considering. In December 1998, New York City Police Commissioner Howard Safir made an announcement that stirred up immediate controversy nationwide. He proposed that DNA fingerprints should be taken not just from convicted violent criminals, but from everyone arrested for a crime. In February 2000, New York Governor George Pataki made a similar proposal. Safir's and Pataki's proposals were not the first of their kind. North Carolina had proposed something similar, and Louisiana was already doing it.

Safir insisted that only the guilty had anything to fear from DNA testing. The New York Civil Liberties Union strongly disagreed. Mere arrest for a crime was no reason to be forced to have your DNA fingerprint entered into the NDIS database. It meant that someone who was only suspected of a crime was being treated the same as if he or she had actually been convicted of a crime.

DNA databases had become an issue that had to be addressed. In March 1999, U.S. Attorney General Janet Reno appointed a Justice Department commission, known as the National Commission on the Future of DNA Evidence. The 22 members of the commission included prosecutors, defense lawyers, judges, police officers, and scientists, all with a thorough knowledge of DNA. They would investigate two issues— whether it was legal to take DNA samples from everyone arrested for a crime, guilty or not, and whether it was advisable. The commission would gather opinions from a variety of sources. The group would weigh the benefits against the risks and make a recommendation by late August 1999.

As with any controversial issue, opinions varied. Some people pointed out that DNA testing was vital to the criminal justice system, not just for convicting the guilty but for protecting the innocent. Others pointed out that such widespread DNA testing would also give the government access to the most intimate secrets of people's lives. If the government were to release DNA information to prospective employers or insurance companies, for example, this would be a serious invasion of personal privacy.

In July 1999, the National Commission on the Future of DNA Evidence issued their recommendation. Yes, they concluded, performing DNA tests on everyone arrested and charged with a crime probably was permitted under the U.S. Constitution. But the commission also advised that mass DNA testing should not begin immediately, because most state crime labs already had huge backlogs of DNA samples that couldn't be analyzed and entered into their databases fast enough to keep up with existing demands.

The problem was money. State crime labs were chronically understaffed. They did not have the funding to hire enough lab technicians to handle the DNA testing and enough computer experts to handle the data.

Meanwhile, the backlog kept expanding. Some 450,000 DNA samples nationwide remained stored and ready for testing, some frozen for as long as 4 years. And more than 500,000 samples still had not been taken from convicted felons in prison. This existing backlog would have to be taken care of before there could be any hope of entering samples from newly arrested suspects. And because some 15.3 million people were arrested in a single year, this would mean that more than 1 million additional samples had to be tested and entered into the database each month.

But even if the backlog could be cleared up, the commission was not sure whether this testing should actually be undertaken. Privacy issues were the problem. As one commission member said, resolving privacy concerns, like how to keep the DNA data from being used to deny insurance, needed further investigation.

New Technologies, New Directions

The problems confronting DNA testing are not going to disappear, but new technologies bring hope of solving some of the problems. One of these problems is time, and another is the mishandling of evidence. Alec Jeffreys' original RFLP testing process could take months to complete. And as the O.J. Simpson trial so dramatically demonstrated, between the time DNA evidence is collected at the crime scene and the time it is analyzed at the crime lab, it can be mishandled so badly that it loses all credibility with a judge and jury.

A forensic *microchip* the size of a credit card and a computer the size of a shoebox may go a long way toward solving these problems. With the microchip, DNA evidence will no longer have to be collected and brought back to a crime lab. Instead, lab technicians can bring the microchip directly to the scene of the crime. There they can place evidence from the crime scene, such as blood or semen or saliva, directly onto the chip, which will then analyze the evidence in a matter of seconds. These chips are capable of performing hundreds of DNA tests at a time.

The resulting DNA fingerprint could then be fed into a computer mounted in a police car at the scene. The computer would be linked to the FBI's NDIS database. In a matter of minutes—and for a cost of less than $20—the evidence could be checked against the national database of offenders. Both devices are being tested for eventual use by law officers nationwide.[10]

But the processing of DNA evidence remains a serious concern for law-enforcement authorities. At present, we have no national standards for DNA evidence collection and testing. The National Commission on the Future of DNA Evidence has been assigned the task of suggesting national standards for the justice system's use of DNA technology. As Executive Director Christopher Asplen says, "The need to guard against contamination, improper storage and handling, and chain-of-custody issues are really some of the most important issues in the effective use of DNA as evidence."[11] Asplen adds that issues of proper evidence collection and avoidance of contamination must be addressed before microchips and other new DNA testing devices can be used in the field.

Law-enforcement authorities are not the only people interested in DNA fingerprinting. During the last two decades of the twentieth century, while forensic scientists were busy developing new DNA testing technologies, scientists in other fields were using DNA fingerprinting for their own purposes. As we shall see, their efforts have left few areas of our everyday lives untouched.

Chapter 6

WILDLIFE PROTECTION AND WORLD HUNGER

Whale Meat on the Menu

A man and a woman sit at a table in a restaurant in Japan. They order raw whale meat, which is considered a mouth-watering delicacy in this country. When their food arrives, they cut it up, but they don't eat it. When no one is looking, the man slides a tiny camera from his pocket. He takes pictures that show both the meat on their plates and the surrounding tables, customers, and staff. Then the woman stuffs some of the whale meat into her purse while the man slips the rest into his coat pocket. No one sees them.

They pay their bill, which is high, because whale meat sells for nearly $60 a pound here. As they leave, the woman places the receipt for the meal in a notebook. Later, she will write the date and time on the page beside it. Outside, the man takes pictures of the restaurant from across the street, and then they hurry away.

In a room at a nearby hotel, two scientists and a video crew await them. When the man and woman arrive, they immediately empty the purse and coat pocket of whale meat. The scientists prepare samples of the meat and put them into sterilized test tubes. They are careful to wash their hands before handling each new sample.

The prepared whale meat samples are placed in a portable minicycler, a machine that uses the PCR process to manufacture millions of exact copies of the whale meat cells. If, as the scientists suspect, the meat comes from a protected species of whale, it cannot be legally transported outside of Japan. But the PCR copies of the DNA from the whale's cells did not come from the whale itself. These DNA copies have been manufactured, so they can be legally sent to a DNA laboratory outside of Japan for DNA fingerprint analysis. The video crew films the entire process.

If the laboratory finds that the DNA fingerprint from this meat matches one from a database of known whale DNA patterns, the source of the meat can be traced. The DNA fingerprint can tell scientists not only what species of whale it is but what part of which ocean it came from.

What good is this information? In 1986 the International Whaling Commission (IWC) banned the killing of nearly all species of whales for commercial purposes. But Japan and Norway have consistently defied the IWC ban, sending huge factory ships out to kill protected humpback whales, blue whales, and Bryde's whales, then selling the butchered meat to fish markets and restaurants in Japan and South Korea. If the suppliers can be tracked down, they can be prosecuted in a court of law.

This entire undercover operation, from restaurant to laboratory, is the brainchild of marine biologists in an organization called Earthtrust, a group located on the island of Oahu, Hawaii. They saw how DNA evidence was leading to the capture of rapists and murderers and decided they could use it to trip up rogue whale hunters too.

Nabbing Poachers and Protecting Grizzlies

The members of Earthtrust are one of many environmental groups using DNA fingerprinting to protect endangered wildlife. Wildlife officials in Canada and the United States use DNA fingerprinting techniques to help nab *poachers*—hunters who kill protected animals for "sport" and, sometimes, for profit.

Lynn Bernard York was a poacher. On December 21, 1998, Florida wildlife officials discovered deer meat in the back of York's pickup truck. Because the truck was parked in a wildlife area where the killing of female deer was illegal, they were suspicious. York claimed the meat came from a buck, which could be killed legally, but University of Florida scientists proved him wrong. They used DNA fingerprinting evidence to show that the meat had come from two white-tail does (female deer). York had to pay a fine of $1,661 and faced a 3-year suspension of his hunting license.[1]

Officials in the Wyoming Game and Fish Department use genetic testing to detect poaching by matching DNA found at the scene of a kill with DNA collected from the suspect's car, home, or weapon.

In numerous other poaching cases, DNA evidence linking a trophy head mounted on a wall or meat packed away in a freezer to piles of animal guts found at the kill site nabs the poacher. "We are actually running the equivalent of a homicide investigation," said the director of the Fish and Wildlife Service's National Forensics Laboratory in Ashland, Oregon.[2]

Wildlife authorities are also hoping to use DNA fingerprinting techniques to catch another kind of wildlife thief. In the Canadian province of British Columbia, $10 million to $20 million is lost every year to tree rustlers who cut down and haul away trees from wildlife sanctuaries. Some of these protected trees are as much as 250 years old and hundreds of feet tall. The rustlers are after money. A single pickup truckload of prime-cut cedar can bring $900 to $4,000.

Just like a person or an animal, each tree has its own unique DNA structure. In catching these rustlers, the idea is not to analyze the criminal's DNA, but the tree's. Research scientists with the Canadian Forest Service have created a databank of DNA fingerprints for individual trees. The RCMP plan to use the databank to match the stump of an illegally harvested tree to the logs in the back of a pickup truck. In this way, even without a witness to the crime, law-enforcement authorities can use DNA evidence to catch the rustler and bring him to justice.

With tree rustling and wildlife poaching on the rise, wildlife officials are stepping up their use of DNA fingerprinting. One DNA laboratory in Ontario, Canada, processes an average of 50 poaching cases yearly, resulting in convictions and fines ranging from $1,000 to $50,000. "We see obsessed hunters," one wildlife official said, "and seasons and licenses don't mean anything to them. It's mostly for ego, and to some extent commercialization."[3]

This is especially true in the case of bears. Estimates put the number of black, grizzly, and polar bears illegally killed every year in North America at 40,000. Some are killed as trophies, but many are killed for their paws and gallbladders. Bear gall fetches high prices on the black market; traditional Chinese medicine uses bear gall to treat a wide variety of illnesses. As with the whales, wildlife officials use DNA fingerprinting techniques to trace the gallbladders that have been seized as evidence back to the species of the bears and the area from which they came.

In the United States, grizzly bears are an especially threatened species. In 1998, wildlife officials estimated that fewer than 800 grizzlies remained south of the Canadian border. Officials have increasingly turned to DNA fingerprinting techniques to help them protect the grizzly bear population in protected areas.

The Greater Glacier Area Bear DNA Project is a case in point. Glacier National Park personnel now use DNA finger-printing to monitor bear populations. In previous years they were forced to use invasive methods, such as collaring and radiotelemetry (the use of radio equipment to collect data at remote points), which meant having to capture and handle the bears, then rerelease them into the wild.

By using DNA techniques, park officials can monitor bear populations without actually coming in direct contact with these wild animals. They get all the DNA material they need by

DNA fingerprinting methods can be used to monitor grizzly bear populations.

collecting grizzly bear scat—animal droppings—and grizzly bear hairs taken from rub-trees—trees that the bears like to rub against. Using the DNA fingerprints obtained from analyzing the scats and hair, park personnel can accurately estimate the bear population in terms of population density (the number of bears living in a given area), sex, and species. In this way, they can keep track of the grizzly bear population and any problems that might crop up.

From Sheep to Rice

What DNA fingerprinting does for animals in the wild it can do for animals bred for commercial purposes. Australian sheep are a good example. Australia is known for its fine wool and, in the world market for wool, high values are placed on pure white fibers. Even a few stray colored fibers can drastically reduce the wool's value.

Merino rams (male sheep) are the source of the problem. Some have genes that produce black fibers, and some don't. The solution is selective breeding through DNA testing. Using low-cost DNA

Ranchers use DNA testing to select Merino rams with the most desirable traits for breeding.

testing kits developed by Australian research scientists, sheep ranchers test their Merino rams before breeding them. The resulting DNA fingerprints show ranchers which rams carry genes for unwanted traits, such as black fibers in their wool. Ranchers then know which rams to select for breeding purposes and which to leave out.

Research scientists in Nova Scotia are hoping they can provide the same sort of valuable information for beekeepers. These researchers have been collecting DNA fingerprints of queen bees for study. They hope to be able to identify the queens with the most desirable traits. Commercial beekeepers could then select these more desirable queens for breeding purposes.

Sheep and bees are only two of many examples. People all over the world who breed living things for commercial purposes are using DNA fingerprinting techniques to improve their flocks and herds and coveys and swarms.

And the people who raise crops to feed a hungry world are doing much the same thing. In the words of J. Perry Gustafson, a plant geneticist, "the world population is increasing at the rate of 96 million to 100 million people each year—or nearly the size of another Mexico City every 12 weeks." Gustafson is dedicated to introducing more genetic diversity into world food crops, such as wheat and rice. Genetic diversity means a greater variety of plants suited to grow more abundantly in more different kinds of environments. "Without being able to identify, increase, and use this diversity, the world could eventually run out of food," Gustafson adds.[4]

Gustafson, from the University of Missouri, along with Zongmin Zhou of the People's Republic of China, have used DNA fingerprinting techniques to distinguish among more than 80 varieties of rice from around the world. Plant breeders can use this database to compare the genetic differences among these varieties. Using this knowledge, they can then select parent plants and seeds with the widest range of genetic variability. The hoped-for results would be the new breeds of rice needed to feed a hungry world.

Chapter 7

WHERE WE CAME FROM, WHO WE ARE

So far, we have dealt with the immediate, active uses of DNA fingerprinting: catching violent criminals and freeing the wrongfully imprisoned; protecting wildlife; and improving the breeding of animals and the growing of crops. All these actions help shape our present and our future. But DNA fingerprinting is also being used to clarify our vision of the past, to reshape history.

History is our accumulated knowledge of the past. But what happens when new facts come to light that add to our accumulated knowledge—or contradict it? To accommodate these new facts, our vision of history must change. Sometimes these changes are welcome, but other times, as we shall see, they cause intense and lasting controversy.

The Unknown Soldier

The Vietnam War ended in 1975 with the fall of Saigon, but, to this day, thousands of U.S. soldiers remain unaccounted for—missing in action (MIA) and presumed dead. On Memorial Day 1984, MIAs from the Vietnam War were honored in a ceremony at Arlington National Cemetery in Arlington, Virginia. The remains of one of these MIAs, killed in Vietnam, were buried there at the Tomb of the Unknowns.

DNA fingerprinting may mean that the identity of the remains of soldiers buried at the Tomb of the Unknowns may be known.

All people knew at the time was that this "unknown soldier" had been killed in 1972 near the South Vietnamese village of An Loc. According to Pentagon records, the remains probably belonged to one of nine MIAs presumed killed in the area. First Lieutenant Michael Blassie, an Air Force pilot whose attack jet had crashed near An Loc on May 11 of that year, was one of the nine MIAs. Blassie's family longed to know whether the remains were those of Michael.

In 1995, when the Pentagon approved DNA testing for MIA remains, the Blassies' hopes rose, and in 1998, under continuing pressure from the Blassie family, the Tomb of the Unknowns was opened so that the remains could be tested. But no existing sample of Blassie's DNA was on record. How could it be proved that the remains of the soldier killed near An Loc in 1972 were Blassie's?

The key was *mitochondrial DNA* (mtDNA). Mitochondria are oval-shaped bodies floating around the nucleus of a cell. A human cell contains only two copies of *nuclear DNA* but thousands of mitochondria. (If all the mitochondria in one human body were laid end to end, they would wind around the Earth 2,000 times.)

While nuclear DNA is a mixture of characteristics from both mother and father, mtDNA is inherited only from the maternal side of the family. It never mixes with DNA from the paternal side. As a result, mtDNA remains unchanged from generation to generation, going back hundreds of thousands of years. If the remains taken from the Tomb of the Unknowns were those of Michael Blassie, the mtDNA fingerprints from those remains would match those of his mother, Jean.

And that's just what happened. The mtDNA tests confirmed what Blassie's family had believed all along, and the remains were returned to the family for burial. As a result, the Defense Department declared that never again would the remains of a soldier be buried in the Tomb of the Unknowns. Thanks to DNA fingerprinting, it is highly unlikely that there will ever be another "unknown soldier."

The Romanov Mystery

The DNA fingerprinting tests on the Blassie remains were performed at the Armed Forces DNA Identification Laboratory (AFDIL) in Rockville, Maryland. The lab's original mission was to identify the remains of Americans killed in war. Its scientists have processed hundreds of cases from World War II and the conflicts in Korea and Vietnam.

They have also worked on so-called "ancient death" investigations, where the remains in question are extremely old and deteriorated. The most famous of these cases deals with a royal family and a mysterious impostor. In 1917, a violent revolution tore apart the social and political structure of Russia. V.I. Lenin rose to power, and Czar Nicholas II fell, ending the 300-year-reign of Nicholas's royal family, the Romanovs. Lenin issued orders that the czar and his family, being held prisoner in Siberia, were to be executed.

In 1920, a woman known as Anna Anderson appeared in Berlin, Germany. She claimed to be the czar's daughter, Anastasia, who had somehow survived the executions in Siberia 3 years earlier. She convinced many people, including distant relatives of the Romanov family, while others called her a fraud. She died in 1964, still claiming to be Anastasia Romanov. The true identity of Anna Anderson would remain a mystery for nearly three decades.

In 1992, bone samples from several corpses were sent to the AFDIL for testing. Unearthed from a single grave in Siberia, the corpses were believed to be those of the czar and his family. As in the Blassie case, the AFDIL scientists turned to mitochondrial DNA to test the badly deteriorated samples. Living descendants of the Romanovs provided blood samples. From these samples, mtDNA was extracted to compare with the mtDNA extracted from the bones of the corpses.

The results showed that the remains were, as expected, those of Czar Nicholas and his family. But what about Anna Anderson's claim that she was Anastasia Romanov who had somehow survived the executions in 1917? Because the case involved royalty and a mysterious identity, a great deal of publicity had been generated over the years, including several books and a Hollywood film. People all around the world still wanted to know whether this "Anastasia" really was a Romanov.

Anna Anderson had died nearly 30 years earlier, but fortunately, a hospital had kept a sample of her blood. This blood sample was shipped to the AFDIL, where scientists performed their tests. They compared Anderson's mtDNA with the mtDNA obtained from the blood of a living Romanov relative—Prince Philip, Duke of Edinburgh and husband of Queen Elizabeth II of Britain. If Anderson truly was who she had claimed to be, the resulting DNA fingerprints would match.

Those who believed Anderson's claim, including some distant relatives of the Romanov family themselves, were doomed to disappointment: AFDIL tests showed that the mtDNA samples did not match. DNA fingerprinting had solved the 75-year-old mystery once and for all—Anna Anderson was not Anastasia Romanov.

Anna Anderson claimed to be Anastasia Romanov, the daughter of the last Russian czar. DNA evidence proved that she was an impostor.

Mrs. Lincoln's Cloak

If DNA fingerprinting techniques could reach back 75 years, could they possibly go further back in history? On the evening of April 14, 1865, President Abraham Lincoln was assassinated. Lincoln was watching a play at the Ford's Theatre in Washington, D.C., when John Wilkes Booth shot him in the back of the head at extremely close range. Mary Todd Lincoln, who was wearing a velvet cloak, was sitting beside her husband when he was

President Abraham Lincoln was assassinated on April 14, 1865, while watching a play at Ford's Theatre in Washington, D.C.

shot. Blood from the wound in Lincoln's head spattered onto Mrs. Lincoln's cloak.

In June 1999, 134 years later, a panel of scientists, conservators, and historians met in Chicago, Illinois. Officials of the Chicago Historical Society had asked these experts to decide whether Mary Todd Lincoln's blood-spattered cloak should be subjected to DNA testing.

Some panel members said yes. If scientists could determine that the blood was Lincoln's, this would prove beyond any doubt that the cloak was authentic, they said. Other panel members disagreed, saying that even with mtDNA testing, it would be difficult if not impossible to prove that the blood was Lincoln's. Because no descendants of Lincoln were still living, there was no one to provide a blood sample for a match.

Some panel members objected for another reason. They believed that the cloak was a vital piece of history and ought to remain always exactly as it was. Why risk damaging the cloak by cutting into it or removing the blood? One panel member was a forensic scientist, and he suggested waiting. In a few years, experts might be able to test the cloak without cutting or scraping it. DNA testing technology would probably have advanced to the point where a simple scan could provide the same results.

After discussing the matter, the panel agreed on a recommendation. There were cases where DNA testing should be carried out, and cases where it should not. In this case, the risks were too great and the possible rewards too small. The society should hold off on DNA testing for now, the panel decided.

Thomas Jefferson and Sally Hemings

In 1802, it was rumored that President Thomas Jefferson, the president of the United States from 1801 to 1809, was having an illicit love affair with Sally Hemings, a woman 28 years younger than himself. The rumors claimed that Jefferson had fathered her sons. Sally Hemings was the illegitimate daughter of Jefferson's father-in-law, John Wayles, and Elizabeth Hemings, one of Wayles's slaves.

Jefferson refused to admit or deny that he had ever had an affair with Sally Hemings. He refused to talk about the matter in public. Whatever his motives, Jefferson had always been a firm believer in the separation of public and private life. He saw it as a politician's duty to never "harass the public with findings and provings of personal slander."[1] Whatever people believed, they did not hold the rumors against him, reelecting Jefferson in 1804 by a landslide.

Thomas Jefferson, the third President of the United States, fathered a boy with Sally Hemings, a slave.

The mystery remained unsolved. Some historians accepted the rumors as true and others insisted they were false. In 1994, nearly two centuries later, a team of molecular geneticists set out to solve the mystery through DNA fingerprinting.

The geneticists focused on the Y chromosome, which passes nearly unchanged from father to son down through the generations. They would obtain DNA fingerprints from the Y chromosomes of Jefferson's descendants and the descendants of Sally Hemings's sons. If the DNA fingerprints matched, a very strong case could be made for Jefferson being the father of Sally Hemings's sons.

The geneticists published their results in the British science journal *Nature*. The tests were conclusive. The Jefferson Y chromosome matched the sample from a descendant of Hemings's son, Eston, so Jefferson had to have been the father of Sally Hemings's son. The results of later tests, announced in January 2000, agreed, and added that Jefferson may also have been the father of her other five children.

When the news was published, reactions were mixed. A great-great-great-granddaughter of Eston Hemings welcomed the news. Julia Jefferson Westerinen had believed it because Sally Hemings was African-American. "There was the element of racial prejudice," Westerinen said.[2]

Jefferson's great-great-great-great-great-grandson Robert Gillespie, expressed the attitude on the Jefferson side: "We're a little bit disappointed that our version of history is apparently not correct," he said. Gillespie was unhappy to learn that Jefferson had fathered Hemings's son. But he was also disappointed that Jefferson had never seen fit to accept Eston Hemings as his son and to give him the same love and affection as he gave his other children. "I guess that was life in the eighteenth and early nineteenth century," Gillespie said, "that they could have children by a slave and turn their back on them."[3]

Reconstructing Human History

If DNA testing could reach back nearly two centuries, how much further back in time could it go? All the way back to the dawn of human history? *Population geneticists* with the Human Genome Diversity Project (HGDP) think it can.

Population geneticists attempt to reconstruct human history by studying the genetic differences among world populations. The goal of the HGDP, an international project, is to find out where and when the first *Homo sapiens*, the first humans, appeared on Earth and trace their geographic movements—and the movements of all the human populations that followed—through time. One population geneticist calls this multimillion-dollar project "the greatest archaeological excavation of all time."[4]

You won't find this excavation site on any mountainside or in any valley on Earth. It lies entirely within the human cell. There, say population geneticists, lies a record of the history of the human species. But reading this record is no simple matter. The problem is not in gathering the information. It's all there, embedded in the DNA of every human cell. Decoding and interpreting this information is the problem.

How do population geneticists decode this information? Their tools are DNA fingerprinting techniques, and their materials are blood samples. HGDP scientists and medical technicians have been trekking all over the world since the early 1990s with syringes and vials to gather samples for testing.

Their mission is similar to the 1987 DNA manhunt when Alec Jeffreys' DNA fingerprinting techniques were first used to solve a crime (see Chapter 2). In that search, blood samples were drawn from 4,583 men in three villages in England over a few months' time with the goal of catching one man, a killer.

The goal of HGDP is far more ambitious, and the time and cost will be much greater. The project will take years and cost many millions of dollars to complete. The scientists plan to analyze the genetic makeup of the entire human population, and from this analysis, to reconstruct human history.

To accomplish this goal, population geneticists must first gather blood samples from a number of people in each of the world's 500 or so *indigenous populations*. An indigenous population is a group of people descended from common ancestors who have lived in the same region of the world for many generations.

One HGDP laboratory, at Yale University in New Haven, Connecticut, has rows of liquid nitrogen freezers. These freezers contain stacks of trays holding hundreds of vials of blood. As more and more blood samples are taken from around the world, more and more vials are added. Each vial is labeled with the name of the

Human Genome Diversity Project (HGDP) laboratories contain blood samples from many groups of people, including pygmies from central Africa.

indigenous population from which the sample was taken.

The HGDP laboratories contain blood samples from people from all over the world. The collection includes African groups such as the Bushmen of the Kalahari Desert, the Baika pygmies of Central Africa, and the Ethiopian Jews. The Asian sample include Cambodians, Malayans, and Tibetans. Samples from the South Pacific include Timorese, New Guineans, Samoans, and Australians. Groups from Europe include Sardinians and Basques. And samples from the Americas include various Native American groups.

However, these samples in the HGDP laboratories are just a small fraction of all the samples that will have to be obtained. Many more must be collected, and collecting them can be complicated because of cultural differences. Western cultures see human blood as simply a physical, organic substance, but some indigenous populations view blood as a sacred substance with awesome spiritual powers. A committee of the HGDP has written about such complications: "In many societies around the world, hair (and blood) is secretly collected from intended victims to harm them through witchcraft. Consequently, people collect their own loose hair, fingernail pairings, and other body products and bury them to avoid this danger." Because of this, "donation of blood in such cultures is a serious matter."[5]

For this reason, among others, the project has drawn harsh criticism. Its severest critics refer to it as "Project Vampire" and want it shut down. Their concerns focus on indigenous populations who are preliterate—they have no written language. Critics of the HGDP ask: How can these preliterate people, to whom Western science is a mystery, possibly understand why they are being asked to donate their blood?

And why should these preliterate people want Western scientists to "read" their blood patterns in order to tell them about their history? These people already have their own oral history, handed down in stories and verses from generation to generation for hundreds and thousands of years. Some preliterate populations, for example, believe that the first humans came from a dark world far below the earth. Don't these people have a right to their own view of human history? What would they gain by being told that their view of human history is wrong?

HGDP scientists are aware of these concerns and address them in their sampling techniques: "Researchers must make full efforts to explain the nature and goals of the project, in the language appropriate for the population and in terms that are relevant to its culture."[6]

Drawing a Picture of Human History

What do HGDP population geneticists do with the blood samples collected from different population groups? They run mtDNA fingerprinting tests on them and then compare the results. They are looking for the mtDNA differences between groups. These differences help lead them back in time. In general, the greater the number of mtDNA differences between two population groups, the longer those groups have been separated.

But how long is long? How can population geneticists calculate the amount of time that population groups have been separated? They use what they call the "ticking of the mtDNA clock," which they measure in terms of mtDNA *mutations*. Mutations are changes that occur in the nucleotide bases in certain genes. These mutations accumulate and remain in the mtDNA, untouched over time. Scientists have estimated that this mutation rate ranges from 2 to 4 percent every million years, meaning that every million years, 2 to 4 nucleotide bases out of every 100 mutate.

What picture of human history have population geneticists gathered from all these mtDNA tests? Think back to the dawn of human history, when the first humans, the first *Homo sapiens*, walked the earth. Picture them as all living in one group in one region of southern Africa. Now picture some of these early humans breaking away into a second group, migrating northward in search of a new place to settle, a new homeland. Then picture other groups breaking away from this second group and migrating off in other directions in search of their own homeland, and so on and so on— until one group living in one place in one part of the world has given rise to many groups living in many places all around the world.

Most population geneticists agree that this is how the original human population gradually spread across the Earth after starting in one part of Africa between 140,000 and 200,000 years ago. According to their estimates, based on mtDNA fingerprinting tests, the first migrating groups reached Asia about 60,000 years ago, Europe about 40,000 years ago, and the Americas about 14,000 years ago.

But this is by no means the true, final picture of human history. As more blood samples are gathered and more mtDNA tests performed, a more complete picture will emerge, and these estimates will change as scientists form an increasingly accurate picture of the distant human past.

Intimate Secrets

We have seen how DNA fingerprinting is used to identify the victims of violent crimes, to catch and convict the guilty, and to free the wrongly accused. This technique can be used in nonforensic ways too—to protect wildlife and to feed a hungry world, to identify the casualties of war, and to reach back into time to rewrite human history.

One last use of DNA fingerprinting remains. It may be the most important use of all, not because of what it has actually achieved but because of what it promises to deliver. This final use of DNA fingerprinting promises nothing less than the unlocking of the most intimate secrets of who we are. It may change our lives in wide, sweeping ways that we cannot yet imagine.

It is a work in progress, called the Human Genome Project, which aims to decode all of the 80,000 or so genes in the human body. Uncovering all these secrets will be difficult. How difficult? Picture a vast display of blinking lights. Think of this display as a single human cell, and think of each light in this display as one of the 80,000 or so genes within this cell. At any one moment in a

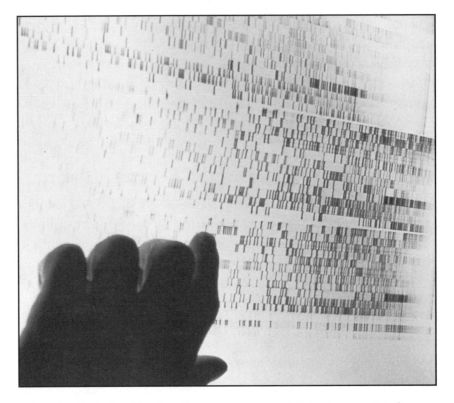

Scientists involved in the Human Genome Project use DNA finger-printing techniques to sequence the genes in human DNA.

typical cell, tens of thousands of genes are turned on and off in a precise sequence to produce proteins. Scientists involved in the Human Genome Project plan to find out what role each gene plays in protein production.

The project will cost billions of dollars. The long-term goal is a longer, healthier life for each of us. The short-term goal is to make it possible for each of us to know our weak points, such as the physical and mental health problems we are likely to encounter during our lifetime—in advance, before they begin to affect us.

Exactly how do scientists plan to achieve these goals? When they have decoded the entire genome, they will know what an ideal, or consensus, genome looks like. In a consensus genome, everything is in good working order.

But no one on Earth has a consensus genome. Everyone's genome differs from the ideal. These differences, or genetic mutations, are like red flags. They signal potential problems. Some of these problems are as relatively trivial as baldness, mild headaches, or occasional bouts of depression. Others are as serious as manic depression, schizophrenia, or heart disease. Genetic mutations in a person's genome signal a greater-than-average chance that the person will suffer from the conditions and diseases associated with these mutations.

On June 26, 2000, scientists in London and Washington, D.C., announced that the first blueprint of the human genome was virtually complete. Some gaps remained, but these would be filled in shortly.

Now the real work will begin. It will take scientists several more years to identify the role of each of these 80,000 or so genes. They will try to find what each gene is used for and the combination of genes it works with to produce certain proteins. When they have succeeded in identifying each gene's role, incidents such as the following may take place.

A mother and father walk into a doctor's office and sit down. The doctor sets before them the *fate map* of their child, Randall.

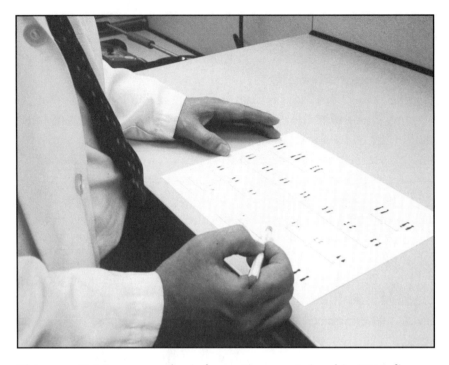

This geneticist can use the information contained in DNA finger-prints to make a person's genetic chart.

This fate map is a summary of the differences between Randall's genome and the consensus genome, and what these differences mean in terms of their child's present and future physical and mental health.

The doctor explains to the parents what the map shows. Although their son is healthy now, certain genetic mutations that occur at certain spots on his genome indicate that he is highly likely to suffer from heart disease sometime after age 40. He is also far more likely than the average person to contract lung cancer if he should ever take up smoking. And beginning in his teen years, Randall is highly likely to feel severely depressed in times of stress.

It's not hard to imagine the controversy this scene suggests, the delicate questions it raises. Should the parents be told these ominous things about their son? Should they tell their son some or all of these things about himself when he grows old enough to understand their consequences? If you had a fate map, would you want to see it?

And what if someone other than Randall or his parents saw his fate map? Imagine Randall at age 21. He's recently graduated from college and is looking for a job. He's also looking for health insurance. What are the consequences for Randall if his potential employers and insurance providers have access to his fate map?

To a limited extent, scenarios such as this one are already taking place. Some employers are already doing limited DNA testing on potential employees to find out who is at risk of developing diseases that would hurt their job performance. If this information falls into the hands of health-insurance companies, they might use it to refuse coverage to high-risk people such as Randall. *USA Today* reported that thousands of people have already been discriminated against because of their DNA. The report states that "Since everyone has at least a handful of faulty genes, no one is safe from becoming part of a new underclass defined by its DNA."[7]

President Bill Clinton took steps to address this problem in February 2000 when he announced an order that forbids federal agencies from discriminating against their employees on the basis of genetic tests. Federal employers are prohibited from requiring genetic tests as a condition of being hired or receiving health benefits. President Clinton announced that he also plans to support future congressional bills designed to provide the same kind of protection to the general public.

Pandora's Box

The controversy over the ever-increasing flood of information gathered by DNA fingerprinting techniques reminds us of the legend of Pandora's box. In that Greek myth, set in an imaginary time when life is all goodness and happiness, the gods give a mortal woman a beautiful box, which they warn her never to open. But overcome with curiosity, she opens the box and out of it fly all the terrible things of the world—sickness, despair, hunger, poverty, and cruelty.

This ancient tale of caution is meant to remind us that curiosity brings new knowledge, and with new knowledge come new problems:

- With a nationwide database, police can compare DNA fingerprints obtained at the scene of a crime with those of millions of potential suspects. But does the entry of those millions of DNA fingerprints into the database violate the civil rights of potential suspects?
- With the help of DNA fingerprinting techniques, population geneticists can tell indigenous people about their history. But what if these indigenous people already have their own ideas about their history?
- With the help of DNA fingerprinting techniques, people will be able to look at their fate maps. But what if the information on those fate maps becomes public knowledge?

The curiosity of the fathers of DNA fingerprinting, Alec Jeffreys and Kary Mullis, did not release a flood of ills upon the world. But it did release a flood of new knowledge and the problems that inevitably come with it. Jeffreys and Mullis looked deeply into what we're made of and found the material that makes us each unique—our ultimate identity. They took pictures of it. They copied it. They helped open the mysterious regions of the human genome for exploration.

GLOSSARY

adenine (A)—a base in DNA that always pairs with thymine

base pairs—the pairs of complementary bases that form the rungs of the DNA ladder

biochemistry—the science that deals with the chemical processes of living matter

cell—the basic unit of living matter from which all plants and animals are made

chromosome—a threadlike structure in the nucleus of a cell that carries hereditary information from parent to child

cold hit—the match that occurs when a DNA fingerprint is checked against a database of DNA fingerprints

cross-examination—the questioning of a witness by a lawyer from the opposing side, to check the truth of the witness's testimony

cytosine (C)—a base in DNA that always pairs with guanine

digital fingerprint—the marking on the inner surface of the last joint of a finger or thumb

DNA—the double-stranded molecule that holds genetic information. DNA stands for deoxyribonucleic acid.

DNA fingerprint—the patterns in a person's DNA. DNA finger-printing is the use of fragments of DNA to identify the unique genetic makeup of an individual.

DNA sequence—the order of nucleotide bases in a piece of DNA

fate map—the record of a person's genome used to determine the likelihood of contracting physical and mental illnesses during that person's lifetime

forensic—see *forensic science*

forensic science—the use of science to obtain evidence for use in criminal trials

gene—the unit of heredity in all chromosomes, encoded to produce a protein

geneticist—a scientist who studies genes

genome—the entire genetic makeup of an individual; the total DNA information contained in all the genes in all 46 chromosomes of a cell

guanine (G)—a base in DNA that always pairs with cytosine

Homo sapiens—the Latin name for a human being

indigenous population—a group of people descended from common ancestors who have lived in the same region of the world for many generations

jury nullification—returning a verdict contrary to law and evidence, sometimes due to a jury's inability to understand highly technical aspects of evidence

microchip—a computer memory-storage device, about the size of a fingernail or smaller, that holds data and instructions

minisatellite—a short fragment of DNA chopped out of a polymorphic region for use in DNA fingerprinting

mitochondrial DNA (mtDNA)—DNA inherited from the maternal side of the family only

molecular biologist—a scientist who studies the structure and function of living organisms on the molecular level

molecule—the smallest particle into which an element or compound can be divided without changing its chemical or physical properties

mutation—a permanent change in DNA sequence that can be passed from one generation to another

nuclear DNA—DNA located in the nucleus of a cell, carrying instructions for the production of proteins

nucleotide—a chemical substance consisting of a sugar, a phosphate, and a base that makes up the rungs of the DNA ladder

patent—(verb) to obtain an exclusive right to make, use, or sell an invention

paternity testing—the process of determining the identity of a child's true father

phosphate—a salt of phosphoric acid; one of the ingredients in the DNA ladder

poacher—a person who illegally hunts or fishes

polymerase chain reaction (PCR)—a method for copying small amounts of DNA for use in DNA fingerprinting tests *polymorphic region*—an area of the genome where the DNA sequence between one person and another shows the greatest variation

population geneticist—a scientist who attempts to reconstruct human history by studying the genetic differences among world populations

protein—one of thousands of kinds of large molecules that are required for the growth and functioning of the human body

public defender—an attorney assigned by a court and paid from public funds to defend people who cannot afford to pay an attorney

radioisotope—radioactive forms of a chemical element with the same chemical properties and atomic number but different atomic weights and physical properties

restriction enzyme—a protein that recognizes short nucleotide sequences and cuts DNA at those sites

restriction fragment length polymorphism (RFLP)—a method of DNA fingerprinting using radioactive probes to detect specific polymorphic regions of the genome

Taq DNA polymerase—a bacterial enzyme used in the *polymerase chain reaction (PCR)* process

thymine (T)—a base in DNA that always pairs with adenine

tissue—a mass of similar cells that performs a specific function; for example: skin *tissue,* muscle *tissue*

END NOTES

Chapter 1

1. Lander, Eric S. "Use of DNA in Identification." Internet page at URL: <*esg-www.mit.edu:8001/esgbio/rdna/landerfinger.html*>.
2. Jeffreys, Alec. "Career Profile." Internet page at URL: <*www.aai.org/genetics/gsa/careers/bro-05.htm*>.
3. Chapman, Tom. "From Antarctica to Chernobyl." Internet page at URL: <*ci.mond.org/9722/972211.html*>. Posted November 17, 1997.
4. Jeffreys, Alec. "Gene Genies." Internet page at URL: <*www.abc.net.au/science/sweek/ausprize/walecj.htm*>.
5. Chapman, "From Antarctica to Chernobyl."
6. Jeffreys, "Gene Genies."
7. Lee, Thomas F. *Gene Future*. New York: Plenum Press. 1993, p. 48.
8. Wade, Nicholas. "Scientist at Work: Dr. Kary Mullis," *New York Times.* September 14, 1998. Internet page at URL: <*www.nytimes.com/library/national/science/091598sci-mullis.html*>.
9. Mullis, Kary. *Dancing Naked in the Mind Field*. New York: Pantheon Books, 1998, p. 7.
10. Ibid, p. 105.
11. Jeffreys, "Gene Genies."

Chapter 2

1. Jeffreys, "Gene Genies."
2. Ibid.
3. Wambaugh, Joseph. *The Blooding*. New York: William Morrow, 1989, p. 71.
4. Ibid, p. 151.
5. Jeffreys, "Gene Genies."

6. Wambaugh, *The Blooding*, p. 167.
7. Coleman, Howard, and Eric Swenson. *DNA in the Courtroom, A Trial Watcher's Guide*. Seattle, Washington: GeneLex Press, 1994, p. 5.
8. Ibid, p. 5.

Chapter 3

1. Lee, *Gene Future*, p. 65.
2. Ibid, p. 64.
3. Zonderman, Jon. *Beyond the Crime Lab*. New York: John Wiley & Sons, 1999, p. 112.
4. Kolata, Gina. "Some Scientists Doubt the Value of 'Genetic Fingerprint' Evidence." *New York Times*. January 29, 1990, p. A18.
5. Lee, *Gene Future*, p. 70.
6. Kolata, "Some Scientists Doubt the Value of 'Genetic Fingerprint' Evidence," p. A1.
7. Levy, Harlan. *And the Blood Cried Out*. New York: Basic Books, 1996, p. 50.
8. Kolata, Gina. "U.S. Panel Seeking Restriction on Use of DNA in Courts." *New York Times*. April 14, 1992, p. A1.
9. Kolata, Gina. "Chief Says Panel Backs Courts' Use of a Genetic Test." *New York Times*. April 15, 1992, p. A1.
10. Coleman and Swenson, *DNA in the Courtroom, A Trial Watcher's Guide*, p. 15.
11. Lander, "Use of DNA in Identification."
12. " 'Not Guilty'." Cable News Network. October 3, 1995. Internet page at URL: <*www.CNN.com/US/OJ/daily/9510/10-03/index.html*>.
13. "Jurors Say Acquittals Were Based on Lack of Evidence." *USA Today*. October 18, 1996. Internet page at URL: <*www.USAToday.com/news/index/nns070.htm*>.

Chapter 4

1. Blakeslee, Sandra. "Genetic Questions Are Sending Judges Back to Classroom." *New York Times*, July 9, 1996. Internet page at URL: <*search.nytimes.com/search/daily/bin/fastweb?getdoc+site+site+39122+1+wAAA+genetic%7Equestions*>.
2. Loeterman, Benjamin (director). *What Jennifer Saw* (video). Arlington, Virginia: PBS Video, 1997.
3. Ibid.
4. Connors, Edward, Thomas Lundregan, Neal Miller, and Tom McEwen. *Convicted by Juries, Exonerated by Science: Case Studies in the Use of DNA Evidence to Establish Innocence After Trial*. Washington, D.C.: U.S. Department of Justice. June, 1996. Internet page at URL: <*www.ncjrs.org/txtfiles/dnaevid.txt*>.
5. Loeterman, *What Jennifer Saw* (video).
6. Possley, Maurice, and Jeremy Manier. "Police Crime Lab on the Hot Seat." *Chicago Tribune*. September 9, 1998, p. 30.

Chapter 5

1. "Certification of DNA and Other Forensic Specialists." Washington, D.C.: National Institute of Justice. July, 1995. Internet page at URL: <*www.nlectc.org/pdffiles/dnacert.pdf*>.
2. Goldberg, Carey. "DNA Databanks Giving Police a Powerful Weapon, and Critics." *New York Times*. February 19, 1998. Internet page at URL: <*hope-dna.com/articles/ha_nytimes_980219.htm*>.
3. Loeterman, *What Jennifer Saw* (video).
4. Goldberg, "DNA Databanks Giving Police a Powerful Weapon, and Critics."
5. Ibid.
6. FBI press release of October 13, 1998. Washington, D.C. Internet page at URL: <*hope-dna.com/docs/fbi_natpress_981013_1.htm*>.
7. Goldberg, "DNA Databanks Giving Police a Powerful Weapon, and Critics."
8. Wade, Nicholas. "F.B.I. Set to Open Its DNA Database for Fighting Crime." *New York Times*. October 12, 1998, p. A1.
9. Ibid, p. A16.
10. Willing, R. "Science at the Crime Scene." *USA Today*. May 4, 1999, p. 4A.
11. "DNA Commission Issues Reports." ABCNEWS.com. September 27, 1999. Internet page at URL: <*abcnews.go.com/wire/US/ap19990923_1470.html*>.

Chapter 6

1. Weis, Lillian. "Deer's Genetic Fingerprint Helps Officers Nab Poacher." *Palm Beach Post*. March 25, 1999. Internet page at URL: <*www.gopbi.com/news/1999/03/25/deerdna.html*>.
2. Sink, Mindy. "Genetic Pawprints Are Leading Game Wardens to the Poachers." *New York Times*. May 26, 1998. Internet page at URL: <*search.nytimes.com/search/daily/bin/fastweb?getdoc+site+site+38864+0+wAAA+genetic%7Epawprints*>.
3. Ibid.
4. Cooke, Linda. "DNA Fingerprinting of Rice Varieties." Internet page at URL: <*www.ars.usda.gov/is/pr/1997/ricedna0697.htm*>.

Chapter 7

1. Chang, "DNA Test Sheds Light on Old Scandal." ABC News. Internet page at URL:<*www.abcnews.com/sections/science/DailyNews/jefferson981031.html*>.
2. Ibid.
3. Ibid.
4. Powledge, Tabitha, and Mark Rose. "The Great DNA Hunt." *Archaeology*. November/December, 1996, p. 37.
5. "Human Genome Diversity Project, Model Ethical Protocol for Collecting DNA Samples." Stanford University. Internet page at URL: <*www.stanford.edu/group/morrinst/hgdp/protocol.html#Q2*>.
6. Ibid.
7. Armour, "Could Your Genes Hold You Back?" *USA Today*. May 5, 1999, p. B1.

TO FIND OUT MORE

Books

Balkwill, Francis. *DNA Is Here to Stay*. Minneapolis, Minnesota: Carolrhoda Books, 1993.

Fridell, Ron. *Solving Crimes: Pioneers of Forensic Science*. New York: Franklin Watts, 2000.

Lampton, Christopher. *DNA Fingerprinting*. New York: Franklin Watts, 1991.

Levy, Harlan. *And the Blood Cried Out*. New York: Basic Books, 1996.

Mullis, Kary. *Dancing Naked in the Mind Field*. New York: Pantheon Books, 1998.

Sheindlin, Gerald. *Blood Trail: True Crime Mysteries Solved by DNA Detectives*. New York: Ballantine, 1996.

Wambaugh, Joseph. *The Blooding*. New York: William Morrow, 1989.

Zonderman, Jon. *Beyond the Crime Lab: The New Science of Investigation*. New York: John Wiley & Sons, Inc., 1999.

Films and Videos

Genetic Fingerprinting (video). Chicago, Illinois: Encyclopedia Britannica Educational Corporation, 1992.

Loeterman, Benjamin (director). *What Jennifer Saw* (video). Arlington, Virginia: PBS Video, 1997.

Niccol, Andrew (director). *Gattaca* (film, video). Columbia Pictures Corporation, 1997.

Organizations and Online Sites

A great deal of information on forensic science can be found on the World Wide Web. Use any Web search engines (Yahoo, Alta Vista, Excite, and others) to call up lists of Web sites. When you do your searches, use key words such as these:

• DNA fingerprinting
• PCR
• genome
• forensic science
• captive breeding
• population genetics

The following is a list of Web sites dealing with various aspects of DNA fingerprinting. Because Internet sites are not always permanent, their addresses may change or they may even cease to exist. The following sites have been in existence for some time.

Crime Stoppers International
www.c-s-i.org/world.htm
A worldwide nonprofit organization that is dedicated to involving citizens with local law-enforcement agencies in order to stop crime in their community. To find the Crime Stoppers program nearest you, look in the phone book.

The DNA Files
http://www.dnafiles.org/about/index.html
Transcripts of nine National Public Radio broadcasts about DNA. Subjects include the Human Genome Project, fate maps, and the use of DNA fingerprinting techniques with plants and animals.

DNA Fingerprinting: a Hands-On Tutorial
http://csdb.nidr.nih.gov/chanchai_site/educ180/nih/DNA_how2.html
DNA fingerprinting techniques, both RFLP and PCR, are shown in step-by-step detail.

DNA Forensics: Crime
http://www.people.virginia.edu/~rjh9u/forenscr.html
A view of actual DNA fingerprints. See if you can figure out which one of the seven suspects' DNA fingerprint matches the one taken from a bloodstain at the scene of the crime.

Evidence: The True Witness
http://library.advanced.org/17049/gather/
Detailed information about DNA fingerprinting and other aspects of forensic science.

The Gene Almanac

http://vector.cshl.org/

A beginning course in genetics, including information on important experiments and animations to explain them.

The Simpson File Transcripts

http://207.175.199.183/~walraven/simpson/simpson.html

Complete transcripts of all nine months of testimony from "the trial of the century," in which DNA evidence was the key, including juror interviews, witness lists, and the verdict.

Stanford Morrison Institute for Population and Resource Studies

http://www.stanford.edu/group/morrinst/hgdp.html

A site that provides a detailed explanation of the Human Genome Diversity Project, with links to related internet sites.

Stanford's Human Genome Education Program

http://www.shgc.stanford.edu

A site devoted to the Human Genome Project for high school and middle school teachers and students to help users "make educated decisions on the personal, ethical, and societal questions raised by the application of genome information and technology in their lives."

INDEX

INDEX

ABOUT THE AUTHOR

Ron Fridell has been writing since his college days at Northwestern University, where he earned a Master's Degree in Radio, TV, Film. He taught English as a second language while a member of the Peace Corps in Bangkok, Thailand. He has written for radio, TV, newspapers, and textbooks. In addition, he is the author of *Solving Crimes: Pioneers of Forensic Science*, published by Franklin Watts. He lives in Evanston, Illinois, with his wife Patricia and their dog, an Australian Shepherd named Madeline.